Our Worship To God

A Look At Man's Obligation And Privilege To Worship God

By
Frank Richey

"Oh, worship the LORD in the beauty of holiness! Tremble before Him, all the earth."
Psalm 96:9

© Frank Richey, 2008
ALL RIGHTS RESERVED. No part of this book may be
reproduced in any form or by any means, without
written permission from the author.

Scripture Quotations

All of the scripture quotations are taken from the New King James
Version of the Bible, unless indicated otherwise.

For the help received in the printing of this book, I wish to thank
Bennie Johns of Baileyton, Alabama
for the pre-press work.

ISBN 978-09816519-0-9

Published by
Cypress Creek Book Company
Florence, Alabama

Dedication

This book is dedicated to my life-long companion,
Julia—the joy of my life and source of
encouragement in all that
is good and right.

Acknowledgements

This book has been the result of sermons I have preached and articles that I have written over the years. I am sure several of the ideas came from those who have taught me and had an influence on me as I have tried to preach. I appreciate the church where I preach for their support, as much of this material was written for the monthly church bulletin and/or was the subject of sermons preached over the past several years.

I have had many people from several states to call, write, or email me, and make kind comments about the material as it appeared in the bulletins. Some have requested material to share with others, and have asked permission to reprint it. Many have expressed that the material was written in a simple, easily understood manner and backed up with scripture. Because of this encouragement, I have decided to make this material available in book form.

A special appreciation is due Harold Young, who more than anyone else, called and thanked me many times for the work in producing these lessons. His encouragement has prompted this writing. I appreciate Harold Comer for sharing the material on worship weariness and Frank Jamerson for his help with the lesson on the contribution as a part of worship. My wife, Julia, is my closest confidant and critic. Without her, I could not have completed this material.

I appreciate Bobby Graham, Lavaga Logan, and my wife, Julia, for the time they spent proofreading and making suggestions for the book. Without them, this material would not be readable.

Table of Contents

Part 1—Our Worship To God
Page

Introduction 6
A Look At Man's Obligation To Worship God 8
Things That Render Worship Unacceptable.............................17
Worship Weariness...24
Sanctifying The Lord Through Worship 32
Hindering Our Worship By Leaving Our First Love 40
Example of An Old Testament Assembly 48
Emotionalism In Worship 56
Women In Leadership Roles In Worship 65

Part 2—How We Worship

How We Worship—Introduction 74
How We Worship—Singing 76
How We Worship—Prayer, Part 1 86
How We Worship—Prayer, Part 2 96
How We Worship—Lord's Supper...106
How We Worship—Preaching...116
How We Worship—The Contribution 126

Epilogue: What The Bible Says About Salvation 134
Final Word..142

Introduction

We live in a modernistic, fast paced world—a world that is materially minded, self-centered, and entertainment crazed. It is a world in which love and respect for God's word have been replaced with what man thinks and feels about worship. This is how man determines whether worship is acceptable to God. But is this the kind of worship God accepts?

God is not like us. His ways are higher than our ways, and His thoughts higher than our thoughts (Isaiah 55:9). Jeremiah tells us, "O LORD, I know the way of man is not in himself; It is not in man who walks to direct his own steps" (Jeremiah 10:23).

It surprises many that acceptable worship is not determined by man, but by God. When we determine to worship as we see fit by leaving off practices we should do in worship and adding practices for which we have no authority, we are, in essence, making God in man's image. So often our concept of worship is, "If I like it, God must like it too."

Through the ages, men have made their gods according to themselves. This is seen in the gods of the Greeks and Romans, as well as the Norse gods and gods of the American Indians. In every instance, the gods reflected the people that worshiped them, and in every instance the worship given to those gods is a reflection, a mirror, of the people themselves.

The tendency to believe that God is like man is as old as the ages and has come to full bloom in the modern world. Many believe that anything they like in worship, God must like also, because He gave them the desires for those things. Our question must be, "What has God said about the way He wants man to worship Him?" We find the answer in the Bible, the God-breathed, Spirit-directed, inspired words of the creator of the universe.

In this study, we want to take the Bible as our authority (i.e., right, power, jurisdiction), and see what God has to say about our worship to Him. When it comes to worship, God wants things done right. This is seen in the first instance of worship recorded in the scriptures when Cain and Abel brought sacrifices to God. God accepted Abel's sacrifice and rejected Cain's sacrifice (Genesis 4:1-8). It is seen again in the first instance of worship under the Law of Moses, when Nadab and Abihu, the sons of Aaron and nephews of Moses, were consumed by fire from heaven for not burning incense to God in the prescribed manner (Leviticus 10:1-3). These examples show that God is concerned about how He is worshiped.

I believe that the material in this book is needed today and needs to be made available to as many as possible in order that we might worship God as He intended. Much corruption of worship today is due to ignorance of the subject of worship. I hope you find this material useful in your service to Christ.

My plea is that man would return to the Bible and do God's things in God's ways. The Bible is the only true source of religious authority. We can either worship in God's way or man's way. The way we worship will determine where we spend eternity.

Since God is concerned about how we worship Him, shouldn't we be concerned about how we worship God? Explore with me the subject of worship as we begin this study.

Chapter 1

A Look At Man's Obligation To Worship God

Recently, a local newspaper carried several articles about a church in a particular area. A local denominational church was employing what they called the "Fear Factor" ministry, based on the television show by the same name in which people are required to do all kinds of disgusting things. It appeared that the higher the ugh-h-h-h factor, the more the people like it. Well, this local church was having as a part of their "Fear Factor" ministry a practice of having the young people to swallow live goldfish! In all the discussion about the church's "Fear Factor" ministry, nothing was said about how we are to worship God. However, the church met its match when the "People for the Ethical Treatment of Animals" got involved. PETA put the pressure on the church and soon we read the headline in the paper: **"Church agrees to stop practice of swallowing live goldfish."** The local spokeswoman for PETA said in the article, "The church wouldn't see fit to torture a dog or cat, and a fish suffers no less than a dog or cat would. Just because they aren't warm and fuzzy doesn't mean they deserve any less protection from harm."

Now I've studied my Bible for fifty years and I haven't found anything about a "Fear Factor" ministry or about the apostles having a service where live goldfish were swallowed. In fact, I haven't found where they brought out a basket of rattlesnakes and handled them as a show of divine authority; but there are still some churches that do that today.

As we witness more and more foolishness in churches today that ascribe various attempts to tickle the senses and especially to "tickle the ears" of members and prospects, it makes me wonder if the concept of worship today is that worship is something that is directed toward men and for men, rather than toward God and for God. Many churches today magnify man (men and women) as they perform and dazzle the audience. I wonder if God feels left out in all of this.

For example, have you noticed the number of churches that are going to a "contemporary worship" alternative? From what I understand of "contemporary worship", it is a worship service that deviates from a solemn honoring of God, and attempts to make those present feel good. Everywhere we see churches delivering the message—"come as you are", "put some excitement in your worship", and "we will accept anybody." (This may mean you don't have to give up your sin to be a part of the church.) Emphasis is placed on the "Praise Team", swaying the body in rhythm with the songs, clapping the hands, and cheering the preacher when he says something humorous or agreeable. More and more churches are magnifying man and minimizing God. What God wants has to take back seat to what men want in their worship to God. Several years ago a man told me, speaking of using instruments in worship services, "I don't care what the Bible says. I like it!" I think this pretty well sums up the concept of worship today. If I like it, who is God to tell me I can't do this?

What Is Worship?

Webster's dictionary defines worship as: "The reverent love and allegiance accorded a deity, idol, or sacred object. A set of ceremonies, prayers, or other religious forms by which this love is expressed. Ardent devotion; adoration." The English word, "worship", means "worthship," denoting worthiness on the part of the one being worshiped. W.E. Vine's Expository Dictionary of New Testament Words gives the following terms about worship used in the New Testament:

Proskuneo- (pros- toward + kuneo- to kiss) It is the most frequent word rendered worship. It is an act of homage or reverence toward God. Some of the passages that have this word are: Matthew 2:2, 8, 11; 4:10; 8:2; 9:18; 14:33; 15:25; 20:20; 28:9, 17.
Sebomai- To revere, the feeling of awe or devotion of worship. (Matthew 15:9)
Sebazomai- To honor religiously. (Romans 1:25)
Latreuo- To serve or render a religious service. (Philippians 3:3)
Eusebeo- To act piously towards... (Acts 17:23)

Vine goes on to say, "The worship of God is nowhere defined in the scripture. A consideration of the above verbs shows that it is not confined to praise; broadly it may be regarded as the direct acknowledgement to God, of His nature, attributes, ways and claims, whether by the outgoing of the heart in praise and thanksgiving or by deed done in such acknowledgement."

As we consider that worship is our moral responsibility, let us consider these definitions:

Our- The possessive form of we. Personal responsibility.

Moral- Of or concerned with the judgment of the goodness or badness of human action and character; pertaining to the discernment of good or evil. (2) Designed to teach goodness or correctness of character and behavior. (3) being or acting in accordance with standards and precepts of goodness or with established codes of behavior.

Responsibility- A thing or person that one is answerable for; a duty, obligation or burden.

Basic Principles Concerning Worship

There are several principles that should determine the worship we offer to the God of heaven. We must realize that (1) Jehovah has the right to prescribe the kind of worship which He will accept. (2) Man has no authority to dictate to God the kind of worship that God will accept. (3) God has always told man how He wants man to worship Him. (4) The only way man can know that his worship pleases God is for God to reveal to man what He wants in worship. We cannot know God's will except through revelation. (5) Since God has revealed to man the kind of worship which pleases Him, we can know what worship God will accept. (6) Two things must be present in order to properly worship. They are: (a) man must respect and adore the one being worshiped, and (b) that respect and veneration must be expressed according to the will of the one being worshiped.

Why Man Must Respect And Worship God

It is interesting that the Greek word for man is *anthropos,* which means **"the one who looks up."** Man was made to look up to a higher power, to respect, adore and worship Jehovah as his creator. Let us look at six reasons why we should respect and adore the creator and worship Him as our God.

God Created Man. God made me and is due my respect and honor, my adoration and worship. "In the beginning God created the heavens and the earth" (Genesis 1:1). "For by Him all things were created that are in heaven and that are on earth, visible and invisible, whether thrones or dominions or principalities or powers. All things were created through Him and for Him" (Colossians 1:16).

God Is Omnipotent. God is all-powerful! He is almighty. "Also, God said to him: I am God Almighty. Be fruitful and multiply" (Genesis 35:11). In Exodus 6:3, God said He "appeared to Abraham, to Isaac, and to Jacob, as God Almighty." If the God of heaven is Almighty (and I believe He is), He has a right to tell us how to worship Him!

God Is Omnipresent. God is everywhere! The psalmist pondered the majesty of God when he wrote, "Where can I go from Your Spirit? Or where can I flee from Your presence? If I ascend into heaven, You are there; If I make my bed in hell, behold, You are there. If I take the wings of the morning, and dwell in the uttermost parts of the sea, even there Your hand shall lead me, and Your right hand shall hold me. If I say, "Surely the darkness shall fall on me," even the night shall be light about me; indeed, the darkness shall not hide from You, but the night shines as the day. The darkness and the light are both alike to You" (Psalm 139:7-12).

God Is Love. I am so thankful that the God I worship is a God of love. How depraved we would be if He was not. The Bible says, "Beloved, let us love one another, for love is of God; and everyone who loves is born of God and knows God. He who does not love does not know God, for God is love. In this the love of God was manifested toward us, that God has sent His only begotten Son into the world, that we might live through Him. In this is love, not that we loved God, but that He loved us and sent His Son to be the propitiation for our sins. Beloved, if God so loved us, we also ought to love one another" (1 John 4:7-11).

God Is Holy. "Holy" is defined as divine; pure; worthy of special respect or awe. Certainly this is true of our God, Jehovah. When Israel turned from God, Isaiah warned about provoking the "Holy One of Israel." "Alas, sinful nation, A people laden with iniquity, a brood of evildoers, children who are corrupters! They have forsaken the LORD, They have provoked to anger **The Holy One of Israel**, They have turned away backward" (Isaiah 1:4).

God Gives Gifts To Men. Not only does God bless us in this life, but He has great things in store for the faithful in eternity. We must live acceptably in order to receive the gift He has in store for us. "For the wages of sin is death, but the gift of God is eternal life in Christ Jesus our Lord" (Romans 6:23). "For by grace you have been saved through faith, and that not of yourselves; it is the gift of God," (Ephesians 2:8).

How Should I Worship God?

"God is spirit: and they that worship Him must worship Him in spirit and truth" (John 4:24). This is what Jesus told the Samaritan woman at the well. True worship consists of worshiping in "spirit" and in "truth." Let us look at what this means.

In Spirit

Adam Clarke, in his Bible Commentary, points out that *"A man worships God in spirit, when, under the influence of the Holy Ghost, he brings all his affection, appetites, and desires to the throne of God."* Clarke also says, *"There is a God...This God can be pleased only with that which resembles Himself: therefore He must hate sin and sinfulness; and can delight in those only who are made partakers of His own Divine nature."* In order to worship in spirit, we must consider the following points:

We should be opposed to all carnality. We must be opposed to those things pertaining to flesh, i.e., bodily, temporal. Paul warned of this when he said, "I fed you with milk and not with solid food; for until now you were not able to receive it, and even now you are still not able; for you are still carnal. For where there are envy, strife, and divisions among you, are you not carnal and behaving like mere men" (1 Corinthians 3:2-3).

We should be opposed to the idea of a God dwelling in temples made with hands. This was certainly the thought of the day concerning the various gods of the Greeks and Romans. They spent great amounts of money to build and maintain places of worship in which they believed their gods dwelled. Paul pointed out that this is not so with the God we worship, when he said, "God, who made the world and everything in it, since He is Lord of heaven and earth, does not dwell in temples made with hands" (Acts 17:24).

We should emphasize the spiritual aspect of worship as opposed to rote, ritual, and form. That is simply going through the motions and checking off each thing we are supposed to do to worship God, without having our hearts in the worship.

We should worship in a way in which the human soul holds intimate communion with the Divine Spirit. "For God is my witness whom I serve with my spirit in the gospel of His Son..." (Romans 1:9); "Praying always with all prayer and supplication in the Spirit..." (Ephesians 6:18).

In Truth

Adam Clarke's Commentary says, *"A man worships God in truth, when every purpose and passion of his heart, and when every act of his religious worship, is guided and regulated by the word of God."* So what does it mean to worship God in truth? I believe the following principles must accompany our worship.

We should worship according to God's word. This simply means we are to worship according to the pattern given in the New Testament. We must accept God's word as truth. Peter says we purify our souls in obeying the truth and it is through the truth that we are born again (1 Peter 1:22-23).

We should respect the authority of God. We respect the authority of God when we respect the right, power, and jurisdiction of God. This concept is reflected in Luke 6:46 when Jesus said, "But why do you call Me 'Lord, Lord,' and not do the things which I say?" The words of the apostle Paul reflect this when he said, "And whatever you do in word or deed, do all in the name of the Lord Jesus, giving thanks to God the Father through Him" (Colossians 3:17).

We should leave the doctrines of men. We cannot worship God in truth if we are worshiping according to the doctrines of men. Jesus warned of such when He said, "These people draw near to Me with their mouth, And honor Me with their lips, But their heart is far from Me. And in vain they worship Me, Teaching as doctrines the commandments of men" (Matthew 15:8-9).

We should lay aside our will and conform to God's will. The real problem in worship today seems to be that men want to worship God "their way" instead of "God's way." The Bible refers to this as "will worship" or "self-imposed religion." Paul mentioned several things the Colossian brethren were doing wrong, and then said, "These things indeed have an appearance of wisdom in self-imposed religion, false humility, and neglect of the body, but are of no value against the indulgence of the flesh" (Colossians 2:23).

We should give God our very best. God has always demanded the very best of His people. He will not accept second-best or leftovers. He wants first place in our hearts. In Leviticus 22:19-24, God spoke of the kind of sacrifice He wanted. The animals sacrificed to God could not have a spot or defect; they had to be perfect; not broken or maimed; no ulcer or eczema or scabs; could not have one leg longer than the others or one leg shorter than the others; the offering was not to be bruised or crushed or torn or cut. If the animal had any of these defects, God would not accept it.

It is strange that the attitudes of many toward worship today is that God will accept any new kind of man-pleasing gimmick that man can come up with to help him in his worship to God. Rock bands, music concerts, and yes, even swallowing live goldfish, are just a few of these new gimmicks.

We should live sacrificial lives for God. The Bible teaches that we are to live sacrificial lives and tells us that we are living sacrifices. "I beseech you therefore, brethren, by the mercies of God, that you **present your bodies a living sacrifice**, holy, acceptable to God, which is your reasonable service. And do not be conformed to this world, but be transformed by the renewing of your mind, that you may prove what is that good and acceptable and perfect will of God" (Romans 12:1-2). John tells us that we cannot love the world and love God. "Do not love the world or the things in the world. If anyone loves the world, the love of the Father is not in him. For all that is in the world—the lust of the flesh, the lust of the eyes, and the pride of life—is not of the Father but is of the world. And the world is passing away, and the lust of it; but he who does the will of God abides forever" (1 John 2:15-17).

Conclusion

From this first lesson we have noticed a number of things about the nature of God and the worship of Him as the Creator of the universe. Keep in mind that God has revealed how He wants to be worshiped and it is man's responsibility to worship God according to God's will, not man's will. When this is done, worship will be acceptable to God.

Chapter 2

Things That Render Worship Unacceptable To God

There are many scriptures that speak of worship that is unacceptable to God. As we consider this subject, let each of us make a personal application of this lesson.

Having the wrong attitude toward a brother- Jesus spoke of this in Matthew 5:23-24 when He said, "Therefore if you bring your gift to the altar, and there remember that your brother has something against you, leave your gift there before the altar, and go your way. First be reconciled to your brother, and then come and offer your gift." Certainly we can see how this would negatively impact our worship. Problems with our fellowman can keep us from worshiping God in an acceptable manner. We must resolve these problems so our worship can be pleasing to God.

Arrogance and pride- Jesus points this out in the parable of the Pharisee and the Publican who went to the temple to pray. The arrogance and pride of the Pharisee is seen in his prayer as he tells God how great a guy he is and that he is not like the Publican. On the other hand, the Publican "would not so much as raise his eyes to heaven, but beat his breast, saying, 'God be merciful to me a sinner.'" Jesus said this man "went down to his house justified rather than the other, for everyone who exalts himself will be humbled, and he who humbles himself will be exalted" (Luke 18: 13-14).

Pretense- Jesus spoke of those who would "draw near to Me with their mouth, And honor Me with their lips, But their heart is far from me" (Matthew 15:8). Notice that Jesus says their worship is in vain: "in vain they worship Me, Teaching as doctrines the commandments of men" (Matthew 15:9).

Ignorance- The apostle Paul pointed out that the Athenians were guilty of "ignorant worship" (Acts 17:23), and Jesus said to the woman at the well, "You worship what you do not know" (John 4:22).

Bitterness and Strife hinder worship- When there is violent dissention or conflict between brethren, this hinders acceptable worship. John says, "...he who hates his brother is in darkness and walks in darkness, and does not know where he is going, because the darkness has blinded his eyes" (1 John 2:11). He goes on to say, "Whoever hates his brother is a murderer, and you know that no murderer has eternal life abiding in him" (1 John 3:15).

Confusion and Division- When there is a lack of peace in a church, something is sinfully wrong. Sadly, this is the case in many churches today. Paul said, "For God is not the author of confusion, but of peace, as in all churches of the saints" (1 Corinthians 14:33). This was a problem in the Corinthian church. Divisions existed over following various preachers and Paul said that they were to "be perfectly joined together in the same mind and in the same judgment" (1 Corinthians 1:10). The psalmist said, "Behold how good and how pleasant it is for brethren to dwell together in unity" (Psalm 133:1).

Form and Ritual- Many of the long established religions today are long on form and ritual and short on a true relationship with Jesus

Christ. Jesus said, "This people draws nigh unto me with their mouth, and honor me with their lips, but their heart is far from me" (Matthew 15:8). There is a big difference between worshiping with the heart and just verbally saying things that have been passed down through the years.

Giving God the Leftovers/Robbing God- God is not satisfied with second place in our lives. He will not accept the leftovers of our lives. This was the case in the days of Malachi when the people were offering to God animals that were stolen, lame and sick. God said that if they were to offer these things to the governor, he would not be pleased (Malachi 1:8). Obviously, if the governor would not be pleased, God was not pleased with their leftovers.

Because of the inferior sacrifices that the people were offering to God in the days of Malachi, we find that God Himself asks the question, "Will a man rob God"? He goes on to say, "Yet you have robbed me! But you say, 'In what way have we robbed You?' In tithes and offerings" (Malachi 3:8). Do men rob God today when the collection plate is passed? What about those who are unfaithful for months or years? They have robbed God of their contribution all that time as well as their service to the Lord.

Serving the Devil- I know it sounds strange, but many think they can serve the devil and serve Christ. Folks want to dabble in sin and show up for worship on Sunday. The words of Jesus when He was tempted by the devil are appropriate: "Away with you Satan! For it is written, 'You shall worship the Lord your God, and Him only you shall serve'" (Matthew 4:10).

Lack of Reverence- When we go through the motions of worship and are not mentally engaged in what we are doing, we show a lack of reverence. Nowhere is this truer than when we partake of the Lord's Supper. Paul said, "For he who eats and drinks in an unworthy manner eats and drinks judgment to himself, not discerning the Lord's body" (1 Corinthians 11:29). He goes on to say in verse 30, "For this reason many are weak and sick among you, and many sleep."

Not Paying Attention During Worship- Many times people show up for worship, but if worship is their intention, they fail miserably. Those who do not pay attention in worship fail to satisfy God and fail to accomplish worship. If you have trouble keeping your mind on the sermon, take notes! If you have a difficult time focusing on Christ during the Lord's Supper, read one of the accounts of Jesus' crucifixion. Work at prayer! Work at singing! Remember Eutychus who fell out of the third story window in a worship service where Paul spoke in Troas (Acts 20:9). Remember the words of the preacher, "Walk prudently when you go to the house of God; and draw near to hear rather than to give the sacrifice of fools, for they do not know that they do evil" (Ecclesiastes 5:1). Remember the focus of worship is Christ and God. Keep focused!

Not Hearing Christ- At the transfiguration, God said, "This is My beloved Son, in whom I am well pleased. **Hear Him"** (Matthew 17:5)! Jesus said, "Most assuredly, I say to you, **he who hears My word** and believes in Him who sent Me has everlasting life, and shall not come into judgment, but has passed from death into life" (John 5:24). In Peter's sermon in Acts 3, he quoted from the book of Deuteronomy, "For Moses truly said to the fathers, 'The LORD your God will raise up for you a Prophet like me from your brethren. **Him you shall hear in all things**, whatever He says to you. And it shall be that every soul who will not hear that Prophet shall be utterly destroyed from among the people'" (Acts 3:22-23).

Hearing Christ should bring about spiritual maturity that will qualify one to teach the word of God. The Hebrew writer said, "For by this time you ought to be teachers, you need someone to teach you again the first principles of the oracles of God; and you have come to need milk and not solid food" (Hebrews 5:12).

Not Doing God's Will- There is a big difference between hearing and doing. Jesus said that those who hear His sayings and do not do them are like a foolish man building his house on the sand, and it is destroyed by the rain and wind (Matthew 7:26-27).

James warned about this when he said, "But be doers of the word, and not hearers only, deceiving yourselves. For if anyone is a hearer of the word and not a doer, he is like a man observing his natural face in a mirror; for he observes himself, goes away, and immediately forgets what kind of man he was. But he who looks into the perfect law of liberty and continues in it, and is not a forgetful hearer but a doer of the work, this one will be blessed in what he does" (James 1:22-25).

Not Presenting Our Bodies As Living Sacrifices- The apostle Paul points out in Romans 12 that we are to present our bodies as "living sacrifices unto God." The only way we can do this is to not allow ourselves to be conformed to the world, but be "transformed by the renewing of your mind, that you may prove what is good and acceptable and perfect will of God" (Romans 12:1-2).

Presenting our bodies as living sacrifices means that we are to separate ourselves from the world. One of the great problems today is that many Christians want the blessings that are in Christ but still love the world and all that it represents. John said, "Do not love the world or the things in the world. If anyone loves the world, the love of the Father is not in him. For all that is of the world—the lust of the flesh, the lust of the eyes, and the pride of life—is not of the Father but is of the world. And the world is passing away, and the lust of it; but he who does the will of God abides forever" (1 John 2:15-17).

Not in Spirit- Jesus said that "God is Spirit and they that worship Him must worship Him in spirit and in truth" (John 4:24). God is a spiritual being. It is the spirit of man that must seek the Spirit of God. To do so, we must have our minds in gear as we worship God.

I have often said that our worship is a "Brain Thing." Just going through the motions of an insincere ritual or form is not acceptable to God.

Albert Barnes' Commentary states, *"Spiritual worship is that where the heart is offered to God, and where we do not depend on external forms for acceptance."* John Wesley's Notes On The Old and New Testaments, says,*"We should worship him with the truly spiritual worship of faith, love, and holiness, animating all our tempers, thoughts, words, and actions."*

Not In Truth- The Lord requires our worship to be in truth. Any false worship will not do. Again, Adam Clarke's commentary states, *"Worship must be in truth, not only in sincerity, but performed according to that Divine revelation which he has given men of himself. A man worships God in truth when every purpose and passion of his heart, and when every act of his religious worship is guided and regulated by the word of God."* Worship cannot be "in truth" unless it is in accordance with God's word. Jesus said, "Sanctify them through truth, your word is truth" (John 17:17). The psalmist, in speaking of keeping the law of the Lord, said, "Blessed are the undefiled in the way, who walk in the law of the LORD! Blessed are those who keep His testimonies, who seek Him with the whole heart! They also do no iniquity; they walk in His ways. You have commanded us to keep Your precepts diligently. Oh, that my ways were directed to keep Your statutes" (Psalm 119:1-5)! May we always strive to worship God in Truth!

Conclusion

As we have noted, there are many things that render our worship unacceptable to God. Let us not be guilty of these things so that our worship might be what God would have it to be. Let us never become lax in our worship to God. Let us always remember that we have a great blessing in this country in that we can worship God without the intervention of government. There are many places in the world where this is not the case.

Worship is a subject that we must be reminded of from time to time lest we forget what worship really is. We need to return to basic Bible teaching on this subject and seek to understand what God has told us about acceptable worship.

Chapter 3

Worship Weariness: The Plague of Modern Christianity

It is Sunday morning already! It seems like we just went to church yesterday. Do I have to go? Can't I just stay home and watch a service on television or listen to one on the radio? Besides, I don't get anything out of the service. The preacher is boring, the song leader is off key, Brother Smith prays too long, and there is no excitement in the worship service.

The sentiments expressed above, though perhaps not verbally expressed, are the views of many in the protestant religious world and in a growing number of churches of Christ. Churches experiencing the fall-out of this attitude are often quick to find a remedy in new and exciting programs (ministries). They include everything from Karate-for-Christ to God's Gym (muscular hulks that entertain kids with their physical powers). They have Wrestling-For-Christ, puppet shows, movies, television programs (including the Mayberry ministry—in which Andy and Barney teach moral lessons), bazaars, rallies, and retreats. They are building gyms as quickly as they can finance them so the kids can play basketball and volleyball and the older folks can play shuffleboard, knit, sew, play cards, and take yoga classes. And then there are the music groups that perform at churches, including "Christian rock bands," and charge a cover charge for those in attendance.

Many of the old established denominations that have embraced instrumental music for a hundred and fifty years can find no reason to deny the youth a "Contemporary Worship Service." Since they made the argument that there is nothing wrong with instrumental music, they endure the upbeat, loud, rambunctious worship of their young, but cannot offer any reason why they should not worship in this manner. They don't like it but they endure it!

Not only are these attempts being made to renew vigor in the worship services, but the churches openly and blatantly advertise "Come as you are!" Don't bother to clean up, dress up or even shape up; we are glad to have you. Certainly this flies in the face of Exodus 19:10-23, where the people were told to make careful preparations to meet the Lord when He appeared in the mountain. I'm sorry folks, but if you expect me to find Christ in any of these activities, you need to change your expectations. **The problem today is that man is worshiping God in a manner that is for man's joy and happiness, rather than worshiping God in the manner in which He has prescribed!** Man is then the focus of worship, not God! All of this that man has invented for worship is because man has become weary in worshiping in God's prescribed way. And friends, worship weariness is a problem that has been around for thousands of years.

Biblical Example

"You also say, 'Oh, what a weariness!' And you sneer at it," says the LORD of hosts. "And you bring the stolen, the lame, and the sick; thus you bring an offering! Should I accept this from your hand?" says the LORD" (Malachi 1:13). From this passage we can see that worship weariness was a problem in the Old Testament. Weariness is defined as tired; fatigued; exhausted; impatient. Just as many were weary of their worship in the days of Malachi, many are weary of their worship today. The weariness of worship during Malachi's day was expressed in their sacrifices. God had always demanded the best of the flock as sacrifices, but the people were then offering sacrifices that were inferior; they were stolen, lame, and sick. God said that they had "defiled" His altar in Malachi 1:7, 12, and then challenged them to give their offering to the governor in verse 8. "Offer it then to your governor! Would he be pleased with you? Would he accept you favorably?" says the LORD of hosts." God asked them in Malachi 1:10, "Who is there even among you who would shut the doors of the house of worship?" God said they kindled the fire on the altar in vain, and that He would not accept an offering from their hands. In fact, their weariness had made God weary of them. "You have wearied the LORD with your words; "Yet you say, "In what way have we wearied Him?" In that you say, "Everyone who does evil is good in the sight of the LORD, And He delights in them," Or, "Where is the God of justice" (Malachi 2:17)?

Worship Weariness Is A Spiritual Sickness

Often times, a prolonged sickness will lead to death. The same is true spiritually, and an analogy is made by Paul when he pointed out that some of those in Corinth who were spiritually sick, had indeed died! Paul, in speaking of the Lord's Supper, said, "For he who eats and drinks in an unworthy manner eats and drinks judgment to himself, not discerning the Lord's body. For this reason many are weak and sick among you, and many sleep" (1 Corinthians 11:29-30). From this we can see how worship weariness is a spiritual sickness. Notice how this sickness develops:

Weakness- First, the church member becomes weak, probably because of a lack of interest in spiritual matters. This may be seen in his dress, language, where he goes, or what he sees. Often, his attendance is sporadic. The number one excuse is that "I've been sick." This is probably true, but the sickness is spiritual, not physical.

Sickness- Secondly, the status of the weak one becomes more serious. This weakness deteriorates into illness that may lead to death if not soon corrected. That's where we come in. We are to "restore such a one" (Galatians 6:1), and "save a soul from death" (James 5:19-20). Many have died without anyone showing any interest in them or attempting to save them. We should be ashamed!

Death- Thirdly, the spiritual sickness, if not corrected, can result in death. While blame can be dealt out to many, ultimately the person died spiritually "...because they did not receive the love of the truth, that they might be saved" (2 Thessalonians 2:10).

Worship Should Not Be Neglected

Because of neglect, a once productive farm is overgrown and is unproductive. Because of neglect, a once fine home begins to leak and rot; widow panes are broken; paint wears away; the door is broken down and the place is vandalized. If we never "keep up" real property, it will diminish in value. The same is true with our worship. If we neglect it, our worship (worthship, i.e., demonstrating God's worth to us), becomes ineffective and worthless. Why should we work at our worship? Notice the following:

Worship Gives Us Strength. The psalmist in Psalms 73 pondered the question, "Why do the wicked prosper?" He wondered why the ungodly not only prospered, but also did not fear death (verse 4), did not seem to have trouble like other people (verse 5), were proud and violent people (verse 6), seemed to have more than they needed materially (verse 7), and even questioned the knowledge of God (verse 11). He didn't understand this "Until I went into the sanctuary of God; Then I understood their end. Surely You set them in slippery places; You cast them down to destruction. Oh, how they are brought to desolation, as in a moment! They are utterly consumed with terrors. As a dream when one awakes, So, Lord, when You awake, You shall despise their image" (Psalm 73:17-20).

Because worship gives us strength, we need to realize that when we worship improperly, we become weak spiritually. We need to remember, when we "play church," God doesn't. In order for our worship to be acceptable to God, we must worship in "spirit and in truth." "God is Spirit, and those who worship Him must worship in spirit and truth" (John 4:24).

Improper Worship Upsets God. When we do not worship God in an acceptable manner, we show disrespect toward God and disinterest in His gospel. This is clearly seen in 1 Corinthians 11:27, when speaking of the Lord's Supper, Paul says, "Therefore whoever eats this bread or drinks this cup of the Lord in an unworthy manner will be guilty of the body and blood of the Lord. But let a man examine himself, and so let him eat of the bread and drink of the cup" (1 Corinthians 11:27-28).

When we worship improperly, our worship is an abomination to God. "The sacrifice of the wicked is an abomination to the LORD: but the prayer of the upright is His delight" (Proverbs 15:8).

Not only is improper worship an abomination to God, but we also weary God by improper worship. As we have already seen in the book of Malachi, God abhors worship weariness. Now look at what God says through Isaiah the prophet: "But you have not called upon Me, O Jacob; and you have been weary of Me, O Israel. You have not brought Me the sheep for your burnt offerings, Nor have you honored Me with your sacrifices. I have not caused you to serve with grain offerings, nor wearied you with incense. You have bought Me no sweet cane with money, Nor have you satisfied Me with the fat of your sacrifices; But you have burdened Me with your sins, **You have wearied Me with your iniquities**" (Isaiah 43:22-24).

Weariness Is Contagious

Have you ever noticed that when one person in a group yawns, others will yawn also? I don't know why this is so, but the same is true with worship weariness. It seems that when one becomes weary, then just like the yawn, others become weary in worship, also. Disinterest in worship has caused many to seek self-satisfaction in worship—to find new ways to make worship appealing, regardless of the authority of God. Preachers have known about disinterest in worship for many years and have adjusted their preaching styles to create certain emotions in the hearers to cause them to feel as though they have worshiped. Some preachers employ various styles of preaching in order to counteract worship weariness. Among these are the following:

Hell-fire and Damnation Style- This style of preaching scares the people in the service so they somehow feel that they have worshiped God. The repeated theme of eternal destruction in the fires of hell become so vivid to the listener that he or she determines to live a life of purity in order to avoid this punishment. While eternal punishment is one of the themes in the Bible, this style emphasizes this theme continually.

Pentecostal Style- This style of preaching gives great emphasis on the end of the sentence with sharp and staccato inflection with a marked change in pitch or loudness of voice. This distinct speech pattern is used to excite the listeners.

Happy Protestant Style- In this style, the preacher's voice is happy, joyous, and uplifting. He encourages the congregation to stand, turn around, and greet those around him or her. While this seems to be a technique for just meeting others, it is a technique to cause the blood to stir, invigorate the brain, and to wake up people. This helps keep them awake through the service.

These are among the several styles of preaching designed to keep people awake in a service that might seem weary to one who is not totally dedicated to God and His word.

Suggestions for Worship

There are several things that individuals and families can do to help in the worship service long before worship services begin. Let us look at some of these:

Learn the importance of preparation. Some fail to look forward to worship with great anticipation. We need to prepare for worship long before the worship hour. This might begin on Saturday night or even earlier. Realize the seriousness of worship. Prepare by working on Bible class lessons, praying, and meditating on spiritual matters.

Eliminate problems in preparation for worship. The anxiety of Sunday morning is felt in the homes of many who attend worship services. Getting up, getting breakfast and getting dressed is a chaotic ritual. There may be children in the home that have to be bathed and dressed, clothes found, shoes looked for, and ties found. Bibles and workbooks must be located. Then there is the mad dash to the car and a fast drive to the building. When worship begins, we are emotional wrecks and can't meditate on the sermon. We need to work to eliminate these problems through planning and preparation. This involves time and effort before 8:00 on Sunday morning.

Work at worship. Worship is not an accident; it is something at which we must work. We need to concentrate on worship, eliminate our daydreaming, and remember we are in the presence of the Almighty God of Heaven!

Practice our worship. Practice is a habitual or customary action or way of doing something; repeated performance of an activity in order to acquire or perfect a skill. This can only be accomplished by working at it. We need to work at concentration on the Lord's Supper, prayer, singing, and shutting out distractions. We need to focus on our worship to God!

Worship at home. Worship weariness in public worship may be a sign that there is no worship taking place in the home. The home should be a place of worship. We need to conduct Bible studies with our families. Parents of young children should make sure they study the Bible together. Children need to learn about God's word. They need to learn to speak to God from the heart in their prayers.

Remember, worship is a privilege. We need to thank God daily for the privilege of worship. There are many in the world that would suffer great hardships and difficulties if their worship to God was made known publicly.

Conclusion

The psalmist said, "I was glad when they said unto me, Let us go into the house of the Lord" (Psalm 122:1). How much better off we would be today if our attitude toward worship was the attitude expressed in this psalm. Worship should not be weariness, but a joy; an attitude of gladness for the opportunity of worship should prevail.

When you think about weariness, think about this: What if Christ's attitude had been, *"I don't think I'll go to Jerusalem this week. I know what they are planning. It is too much work, worry, and weariness to die on the cross for these people that can't even come to worship me."*

The next time you think worship is so-o-o-o-o boring; ask yourself how much time, preparation, study, prayer, and meditation went into the worship service on your behalf. If you are not what you should be, then be what you ought to be.

Chapter 4

Sanctifying The Lord Through Worship

In order to properly worship God, we must live a life of sacrifice to God. Paul said, "I beseech you therefore, brethren, by the mercies of God, that you present your bodies a living sacrifice, holy, acceptable to God, which is your reasonable service" (Romans 12:1). The idea of sanctifying is the idea of setting apart, cleansing, making holy and glorifying God in our lives. God demands this of us if we are to be pleasing to Him. Worship, we must remember, is about God. Let us never get to the point where we make man and his doctrines the center of worship. This is vain worship (Mathew 15:9).

Under the Old Law, the priest and vessels had to be cleansed and set apart (sanctified) for the Lord. By doing this, they were made fit and proper for the exclusive use of the Lord. God said, "I will be sanctified in you before the heathen" (Ezekiel 20:41), and "...I will sanctify My great name, which has been profaned among the nations, which you have profaned in their midst; and the nations shall know that I am the LORD," says the Lord GOD, "when I am hallowed in you before their eyes" (Ezekiel 36:23).

The Bible teaches us that Christians are cleansed, i.e., set apart or sanctified. Paul said that the members of the church in Corinth were sanctified: "To the church of God which is at Corinth, to those who are **sanctified in Christ Jesus, called to be saints**, with all who in every place call on the name of Jesus Christ our Lord, both theirs and ours" (1 Corinthians 1:2). In order to be pleasing to God, our worship must reflect these attitudes. If we do not give God a special place in our hearts as we are worshiping Him; if we do not glorify Him and recognize His holiness; then we have failed to sanctify the Lord and we have failed in our worship.

Why Sanctify The Lord God In Our Hearts?

Holy Spirit commands it. We must sanctify the Lord God in our hearts because the Holy Spirit commands it. We should not be guilty of giving God a little corner of our lives. Many people do, and, as a result, do not sanctify God in their hearts. Through inspiration of the Spirit, Peter said: "But **sanctify the Lord God in your hearts**, and always be ready to give a defense to everyone who asks you a reason for the hope that is in you, with meekness and fear" (1 Peter 3:15). We sanctify God when we give Him first place in our lives. Jesus said, "But seek first the kingdom of God and His righteousness, and all these things shall be added to you" (Matthew 6:33).

God Is. The very nature of God demands sanctification as we come before His throne in worship. This concept of "I AM" was one that the Jews understood. When Jesus said, "Most assuredly, I say to you, before Abraham was, I AM", the Jews immediately referenced this to the essential nature of deity mentioned in the Old Testament and took up stones to stone Jesus (John 8:58-59). When Moses requested of the LORD that He tell him who He was, the LORD said, "I AM WHO I AM." And He said, 'Thus you shall say to the children of Israel, I AM has sent me to you'" (Exodus 3:14). The phrase "I AM" carries with it significant meaning. It means self-existent, self-sufficient, all sufficient, and eternal. It means the original being; the same yesterday, today and tomorrow.

God Is The Source of All Good. God must be sanctified in our worship because of the blessings that flow from His throne of grace. James said, "Every good gift and every perfect gift is from above, and comes down from the Father of lights, with whom there is no variation or shadow of turning" (James 1:17). We must never forget that God is our refuge and our fountain of blessing.

He Is Our Hope Beyond The Grave. Hope is defined as desire plus expectation. The hope of Christians is eternal life in heaven. Our hope is often expressed when we quote the most recognizable verse in the Bible, which says, "...God so loved the world that He gave His only begotten Son, that whoever believes in Him should not perish but have everlasting life" (John 3:16). Peter recognized the power of God's word when he said, "Lord, to whom shall we go? You have the words of eternal life" (John 6:68).

God Is To Be Glorified In Worship. The word "glory" means to magnify, extol praise, to ascribe honor. Certainly, this should be expressed in our worship to God. Peter said that, as we speak the oracles (words) of God, God is "glorified through Jesus Christ, to Whom be praise and dominion forever and ever. Amen" (1 Peter 4:11).

Biblical Examples of Those Who Did Not Sanctify God

Obviously, there are many examples of people in the Bible that did not glorify and honor God. Often God was not glorified in worship. This is true whenever man does things his way instead of God's way.

Nadab and Abihu- Certainly this is seen in the story of Nadab and Abihu, the sons of Aaron the High Priest, offering incense before the LORD. When they lit the fire to offer incense, they did not light it from the fire that God Himself had lit. Thinking, no doubt, that fire is fire and that it was "no big deal," they offered "strange fire" before the LORD, "which He commanded not." As a result of this, fire went out from heaven and devoured them. Moses then spoke to

Aaron and said, "This is what the LORD spoke, saying: "By those who come near Me I must be regarded as holy; And before all the people **I must be glorified**" (Leviticus 10:3). We can see from this example that these men worshiped God in the wrong manner, and that if we worship God in the wrong manner, we are not glorifying God.

Moses Striking The Rock- The journey through the wilderness must have been far more difficult than we can imagine. The constant moving about, unbearable heat, the lack of fruit and vegetables, and most importantly, the lack of water, convinced many of the children of Israel that God had led them into the wilderness to die. Though many of them had seen the miracles of God in the parting of the Red Sea and the destruction of the Egyptian army, they still murmured and complained to Moses and Aaron, asking why God had led them so far, only to kill them in the desert. Moses came before God and sought a solution to the problem of no water. God told Moses to gather the congregation together and speak to a particular rock, and that water would come forth from the rock to supply them and their animals with water. The Bible tells us that Moses assembled the people and said, "'...Hear now, you rebels! Must we bring water for you out of this rock?' Then Moses lifted his hand and struck the rock twice with his rod; and water came out abundantly, and the congregation and their animals drank" (Numbers 20:10-11).

Perhaps most people today would not think anything about what Moses did, but the truth is that Moses disobeyed God. God said to speak to the rock and Moses struck the rock. Notice God's response to what Moses did: "Then the LORD spoke to Moses and Aaron, 'Because you did not believe Me, to hallow Me in the eyes of the children of Israel, therefore you shall not bring this assembly into the land which I have given them'" (Numbers 20:12). The King James Version says, "Because **ye believed me not, to sanctify me** in the eyes of the children of Israel..." Continuing to read this passage, we see that as a result of not "sanctifying" or "hallowing" God, Moses was not allowed to enter the Promised Land. Friends, it is serious business when we fail to sanctify God!

The Gentiles- When Paul wrote the book of Romans, he spoke in chapter 1 of the sins of the Gentiles. They had failed to glorify or sanctify God. Paul said, "…although they knew God, **they did not glorify Him as God**, nor were thankful, but became futile in their thoughts, and their foolish hearts were darkened. Professing to be wise, they became fools, and **changed the glory of the incorruptible God** into an image made like corruptible man—and birds and four-footed animals and creeping things" (Romans 1:21-23). Do you think God would allow such blatant disrespect and ungodliness to go unnoticed? Paul says, speaking of the fate of those who did not glorify God, that they, "who, knowing the righteous judgment of God, that those who practice such things are deserving of death, not only do the same but also approve of those who practice them" (Romans 1:32). There is no hope at all for those who fail to sanctify, glorify, and hallow God. The only thing they have to look toward is the vengeance of God and they "shall be punished with everlasting destruction from the presence of the Lord and from the glory of His power" (2 Thessalonians 1:9).

Many Today Do Not Sanctify God In Worship

A gross failure to sanctify God in worship today has yielded a kaleidoscope of worship patterns. And like the kaleidoscope which changes with every movement of the scope, men change their worship to better meet their own needs, rather than the requirements set forth by the God of heaven. The reason man tries to improve on God's plan is that man has a sinful heart rather than a sanctified heart! James said, "Pure religion and undefiled before God and the Father is this, to visit the fatherless and widows in their affliction, and to keep himself unspotted from the world" (James 1:27). Not only do we as Christians have a responsibility to help and relieve those in need, we have the responsibility of remaining "unspotted from the world." A failure to do so will result in a failure to sanctify God. A failure to sanctify God will lead to hell (Romans 1:32). Let us look at some who do not sanctify God in worship.

Those Who Change Worship For Personal Demands- Some are not satisfied with God's plan. Instead of accepting that baptism is for the remission of sins (Mark 16:15-16), they say "baptism is an outward sign of an inward experience." They change immersion of the baptismal candidate to sprinkling or pouring, and thereby deny the example of New Testament baptism (Acts 8:38-39).

Those Who Fail To Share the Gospel- Often we sing, "I want to be a soul winner for Jesus," but often we mean, "I want someone else to be a soul winner for Jesus." A failure to share the gospel is a sign that God is not sanctified in the heart. Jesus said, "Go therefore and make disciples of all the nations, baptizing them in the name of the Father and of the Son and of the Holy Spirit, teaching them to observe all things that I have commanded you; and lo, I am with you always, even to the end of the age. Amen" (Matthew 28:19-20).

Those Who "Play Church" Instead of Sanctifying God- We use the expression, "Playing Church" for one who pretends to be worshiping, but in actuality, he is being hypocritical. Notice the rules for playing church:

Rules for Playing Church

For those who enjoy playing church, consider the following rules that are offered to make your playing more enjoyable. (Keep in mind that we are not advocating playing church, just observing what might happen if playing church was actually a game.)

1. Playing church is played with two or more players. Players will forthwith be called members.

2. Members assemble themselves together 1 to 3 times per week.

This depends on how avid a member you are and how much you feel the need to play.

3. Enjoyment in playing (assembling) is classified as follows: (A) Wearing new clothes so that one member can impress other members with his or her wealth and/or taste in clothing. (B) Impressing others with your knowledge of the Bible. (C) Enjoying the social gathering of the people from the community. (D) Trying to find fault with the preacher, song leader, Bible class teacher or anyone who is willing to take an active role in the service.

4. Members should not study their lessons. This is closely akin to work and not conducive to playing church.

5. Members should not visit the sick, read their Bibles, care for those in need, or talk to the lost about their souls. This too, is work, and takes all the fun out of the game.

6. For those who really enjoy playing, miss several services and think up excuses for why you didn't come. Share these excuses with others so they might use them also.

7. When playing church, be sure to participate in all the items of worship that are required but do not, by any means, give to the contribution, pay homage to God, meditate on spiritual things or try to commune with God. Other members will think you are too serious to play church.

8. For those who would like to excel in this game, live like the devil and be a bad example for others. However, if the subject of religion should come up in a conversation, immediately tell others that you are a member of the Church and argue that they are going to hell if they don't come over and play your way.

This game may be a lot of fun for some, but oddly enough there are no winners. In fact, everyone loses. You lose your time, your example, and your soul. The only thing you can look forward to is eternity in hell with those who played church with you.

Conclusion

Friends, isn't it time we got serious about our worship? Isn't it time for us to scrap all the worship inventions of men, and do things God's way instead of man's way. The Proverbs writer said, "There is a way [that seems] right to a man, But its end [is] the way of death" (Proverbs 16:25). Moses said, "And you shall do [what is] right and good in the sight of the LORD, that it may be well with you..." (Deuteronomy 6:18). Jesus said, "But seek first the kingdom of God and His righteousness..." (Matthew 6:33). Until we sanctify God in our worship and in our lives, we will never be seeking God first!

Consider These Words of the Psalmist

"Give to the LORD, O families of the peoples, Give to the LORD glory and strength. Give to the LORD the glory due His name; bring an offering, and come into His courts. Oh, worship the LORD in the beauty of holiness! **Tremble before Him**, all the earth. Say among the nations, "The LORD reigns; the world also is firmly established, It shall not be moved; He shall judge the peoples righteously." Let the heavens rejoice, and let the earth be glad; Let the sea roar, and all its fullness; Let the field be joyful, and all that is in it. Then all the trees of the woods will rejoice before the LORD. For He is coming, for He is coming to judge the earth. He shall judge the world with righteousness, and the peoples with His truth" (Psalm 96:7-13).

Chapter 5

Hindering Our Worship By Leaving "Our First Love"

If we are concerned about our worship, we must of necessity be concerned about our relationship with Jesus Christ. Jesus should be our "first love", and when anything or anyone takes the place of that "first love", our relationship with Christ is not what it ought to be. As we study this lesson, let us examine ourselves as to our relationship with The Christ.

A look at the condition of the church at Ephesus in the Revelation letter gives a clear indication that the Ephesian brethren were hindered in their work and worship of the Lord. Jesus Himself said, "I know your works, your labor, your patience, and that you cannot bear those who are evil. And you have tested those who say they are apostles and are not, and have found them liars; and you have persevered and have patience, and have labored for My name's sake and have not become weary. Nevertheless I have this against you, that **you have left your first love.** Remember therefore from where you have fallen; repent and do the first works, or else I will come to you quickly and remove your lampstand from its place—unless you repent" (Revelation 2:2-5).

Christ Knew The Church At Ephesus

Jesus said, "I know" (Revelation 2:2). He knew the situation at Ephesus. He was aware of the church, its worship, and its activities. Jesus knows everything. Psalm 139:7-12 tells us that He knows everything there is to know about us. Please notice:
"If I say, 'Surely the darkness shall fall on me, Even the night shall be light about me; Indeed, the darkness shall not hide from You, but the night shines as the day; The darkness and the light are both alike to You'" (Psalm 139:11-12). What did Jesus know about the church at Ephesus? Let us look.

I know your works. Perhaps this refers to the general conduct of the Ephesians, rather than the deeds of the Ephesian church.

I know your labors. Jesus knew of their toil (excessive labor) for the Lord, even to the point of suffering.

I know your patience. The Ephesians were steadfast in their endurance in what was right, even though false teachers abounded. They fought against false teaching and error.

I know you cannot bear evil and false teachers, having tested them. Paul had warned the Ephesians in Acts 20:28 that false teachers would come in "not sparing the flock" and warned the elders to stand against them. Evidently, they did. Jesus commends the church for defending the truth against the error that was being taught without growing weary.

But, even with these commendations, Jesus had one condemnation of the Ephesian church. Jesus said, "...I have one thing against you, that you have left your first love" (Revelation 2:4). Their only hope was to "repent and do the first works, or else I will come to you quickly and remove your lampstand from its place—unless you repent" (verse 5).

How Is Worship Affected By Leaving Our "First Love"?

When a church leaves its first love, the worship of the church is impacted negatively and profoundly. Let us look at some of the disastrous results.

Division Among Brethren- Division in a congregation shows without a doubt that there is something wrong within and that there needs to be immediate correction. Division definitely impedes worship. Paul urged the church in Corinth to be "perfectly joined together in the same mind and in the same judgment" (1 Corinthians 1:10). In saying this, Paul asks the rhetorical question, "Is Christ divided?" Paul, in Romans 15:5, said that they were to be "likeminded one toward another according to Christ Jesus." Jesus, in the garden before His arrest, prayed "that they all may be one; as You, Father, are in Me, and I in You; that they also be one in Us, that the world may believe that You sent Me" (John 17:21).

A Lack Of Love For Each Other- The Bible teaches that there is a connection between loving each other and worship. John says, "Whoever does not practice righteousness is not of God, nor *is* he who does not love his brother" (1 John 3:10). Not having the proper love toward our brethren impedes our worship of deity and can negatively affect our relationship with Christ. John said, "But he who hates his brother is in darkness and walks in darkness, and does not know where he is going, because the darkness has blinded his eyes" (1 John 2:11). He also said, "Whoever hates his brother is a murderer, and you know that no murderer has eternal life abiding in him" (1 John 3:15). He also said, "Beloved, if God so loved us, we also ought to love one another" (1 John 4:11).

An Unwillingness To Forgive- Forgiveness is a basic tenet of Christianity. Many are in adversarial situations today because they are unwilling to forgive, and/or seek reconciliation. When these situations exist between brethren, true worship is all but impossible. Jesus, in the Sermon on the Mount, said, "Therefore if you bring your gift to the altar, and there remember that your brother has something against you, leave your gift there before the altar, and go your way. First be reconciled to your brother, and then come and offer your gift" (Matthew 5:23-24). Forgiveness is not a mere suggestion on the part of Christ, but a commandment. Inspired by the Holy Spirit, Paul wrote, "bearing with one another, and forgiving one another, if anyone has a complaint against another; even as Christ forgave you, so you also must do" (Colossians 3:13).

A Lack Of Zeal- Zeal is defined as earnest enthusiasm as displayed in action; involvement; eagerness in favor of a person or cause. Christians are to have zeal, but the proper kind of zeal. The Romans had "a zeal of God, but not according to knowledge" (Romans 10:2). True zeal in worship is the dedicated, consecrated devotion and adoration of Jehovah as God Almighty, His Son Jesus the Christ, and the Holy Spirit. This adoration can be felt without overt emotional displays of shouting, clapping, swaying, swooning, falling out, and jabbering in an unintelligible manner. We not only demonstrate our zeal by our public worship, but in our daily lives. Paul said we are a "special people, zealous of good works" (Titus 2:14).

Zeal is exhibited by action, by doing. Zeal is contagious. Zeal is not hidden.

How Can We Demonstrate That We Have Not Left Our First Love?

Love is most often used as a verb. Love is demonstrated, not just something you feel or say. We show love, not by telling someone we love them, but by the things we do for them. We need to demonstrate our love to God. This can be done in many ways.

We Must Attend Worship Services. An empty pew speaks reams about a person's relationship to God. When one neglects to assemble with the saints, he or she has determined that there is something more important in their lives than worshiping God. The Hebrew writer tells us, "not forsaking the assembling of ourselves together, as is the manner of some, but exhorting one another, and so much the more as you see the Day approaching" (Hebrews 10:25).

We Must Support The Worship Of The Church. Christians are to be involved in the church of Christ. We can do this by participating in worship. We need to become a vital part of the worship service, remembering that worship is not a spectator sport. When the church sings, we need to concentrate on the words of the song, and actually SING! Singing in worship is not to be for our entertainment. It is done to the Lord and for our teaching and admonition (Colossians 3:16). When we pray, don't allow the mind to take a mini-vacation. Focus on what is being said by the one leading the prayer. When the preacher speaks, pay attention to the message. Allow it to penetrate the heart to bring about spiritual change and spiritual betterment in our lives. When we give, we are to do so cheerfully and bountifully (2 Corinthians 9:6-7). When it is time for the Lord's Supper, we need to be prepared spiritually to commune with Christ. This period of time is perhaps the closest one can come to being with Christ on earth! During this time, we need to focus on the sacrifice that Christ made for us and give ourselves a spiritual examination. Paul said, "But let a man examine himself, and so let him eat of the bread and drink of the cup" (1 Corinthians 11:28).

We Need To Study Our Bibles. It is only by studying our Bibles that we can truly appreciate the gift of salvation and know how we are to serve and worship God. A failure to do so will cause one to be ignorant of God's will and invariably lead to worship that is vain, or to no worship at all. Paul says we are to "study to show ourselves approved to God" (2 Timothy 2:15), and James says we are to receive the "implanted word which is able to save your souls" (James 1:21). Jesus said "He who rejects me and does not receive my words, has that which judges him—the word that I have spoken will judge him in the last day" (John 12:48). John writes that the "dead were judged according to the things written in the books" (Revelation 20:12). In order to worship God acceptably, it is imperative that we know His will, understand His nature, and glorify His name in worship acceptable to Him.

We Need To Be Proper Examples To Others. Jesus said, "You are the light of the world. A city that is set on a hill cannot be hidden. Nor do they light a lamp and put it under a basket, but on a lampstand, and it gives light to all who are in the house. Let your light so shine before men, that they may see your good works and glorify your Father in heaven" (Matthew 5:14-16). Jesus is talking about being proper examples to others. As children of God, we should let others see that there is something special about us. Several years ago this writer talked to a young lady who was interested in being baptized. She was working for two women who were members of the church where I preached. When I asked her why she wanted to be baptized, she said, "I want what they (the two women) have". This young lady recognized that there was something special about the Christian women! This is accomplished by letting our lights shine, not shining our lights (as many do). We do not have to wear a button saying, "I'm a Christian." Just live the life prescribed by Christ for His followers.

We Need To Care For Others. Perhaps we need to ask ourselves, "Are we really concerned about others?" "Do we express our concerns to them, to others, and to God?" True concern for others is quickly detected. This writer spent thirty-one years in public education and can tell you without a doubt that kids in the classroom know whether the teacher cares about them or is just there for a paycheck. The old saying, *"They don't care what you know until they know that you care"* is a fundamental truth. Paul said, "Therefore, as we have opportunity, let us do good to all, especially to those who are of the household of faith" (Galatians 6:10).

So often we condemn others rather than care for them. We seem to have so little patience with others but expect others to have great patience with us. We need to try to understand others and look at things from their perspective to better understand. (That's what the old saying, "Walk a mile in his shoes" means.) As Christians, we are to "Bear one another's burdens, and so fulfill the law of Christ" (Galatians 6:2), and "We then who are strong ought to bear with the scruples (infirmities-KJV; failings-RSV) of the weak, and not to please ourselves" (Romans 15:1).

We Need To Show Love And Concern For The Souls Of Others. Three times in the gospels we find recorded the statement of Jesus about the harvest being great and the laborers being few (Matthew 9:37-38; Luke 10:2; John 4:35). These references are concerning the souls that need to be harvested (saved) for the Lord. The greatest thing you can ever do for another human is to lead him to Christ. This will never be accomplished without trying. If every member of the church would convert one person, the church would double in number. We need to be busy sharing the gospel with others so they may have eternal life.

We Need To Be Willing To Give Reasons For Our Beliefs. Christians should prepare themselves to be ready to give answers to those who question their beliefs. We need to honestly ask ourselves, "If I cannot give someone the Bible verses and show someone how to become a Christian, can I really expect to go to heaven?" We need to properly prepare ourselves for this most important aspect of the Christian life. Peter tells us we are to be able to defend the faith: "But sanctify the Lord God in your hearts, and always be ready to give a defense to everyone who asks you a reason for the hope that is in you, with meekness and fear" (1 Peter 3:15).

Children Need To Be Taught. Young parents should be excited about the spiritual development of their children. Home Bible studies are an important part of the proper spiritual development of a child. One of the greatest joys in this life is to see your own child obey the gospel. One of the greatest sorrows that is experienced by Christians is to see their children grow to adulthood and never become a Christian, or to see their child leave the Lord for the ways of the world. Parents have their role in spiritual development of children as seen in Ephesians 6:4: "And you, fathers, do not provoke your children to wrath, but bring them up in the training and admonition of the Lord."

Conclusion

Hebrews 12:2 tells us that Jesus Christ is the "author and finisher of our faith." That means He wrote it and paid for it. Christianity without Christ is like a well without water. There is nothing there for you. If we lose our First Love, we have quit seeking "first the kingdom of God and His righteousness" (Matthew 6:33). If we lose our First Love, we also lose eternal life where our First Love waits for those that have put Him first in their lives.

Chapter 6

Example of an Old Testament Assembly

The book of Nehemiah is one of the great Old Testament books that tell of the history of the people of God. Nehemiah, the cupbearer to King Artaxerxes, was a captive in Babylon. Upon hearing that a fellow Jew by the name of Hanani, had recently come from Judea, Nehemiah inquired about the situation there. The news of a destroyed Jerusalem with broken walls was alarming and saddening to Nehemiah—so much so that his depression was observable by the king. When asked why he was sad, Nehemiah told of the condition of his homeland. King Artaxerxes, touched by Nehemiah's sadness, made arrangements for Nehemiah to return to Jerusalem to rebuild the walls of the city. After much conflict and hard work at Jerusalem, the walls were rebuilt in fifty-two days (Nehemiah 6:15).

After the repairing of the wall around Jerusalem had been finished, Nehemiah and Ezra gathered the people together to read God's word. For seven days, every day from early morning until midday, Ezra and his helpers read and explained the law of God. This brought a great wave of repentance and revival of faith among the people. On the eighth day, "there was a sacred assembly, according to the prescribed manner" (Nehemiah 8:18).

Notice what the Bible says: "Now all the people gathered together as one man in the open square that [was] in front of the Water Gate; and they told Ezra the Scribe to bring the Book of the Law of Moses, which the LORD had commanded Israel. So Ezra the priest brought the Law before the assembly of men and women and all who [could] hear with understanding on the first day of the seventh month. Then he read from it in the open square that [was] in front of the Water Gate from morning until midday, before the men and women and those who could understand; and the ears of all the people [were attentive] to the Book of the Law" (Nehemiah 8:1-3).

I believe there are several lessons that can be learned about our assembly and our worship today by looking at this Old Testament passage.

The Assembly Was Not In A Hurry To Conclude

Most people today expect the preacher to keep his remarks well within line of the thirty-minute time frame allotted him to speak during worship services. We need to realize that this was not a thirty-minute sermon. This session lasted probably six hours, for seven days, and there was a lot of reading. Often today, it is hard to keep the attention of folks when a long passage from the Bible is read. Imagine reading all that God had to say! Did you notice in Nehemiah 8:3, that "the people [were attentive] to the Book of the Law."

This assembly was much like the Bereans in the New Testament. The scripture tells us that they, unlike the Thessalonians, "received the word with all readiness and searched the scriptures daily [to find out] whether these things were so" (Acts 17:11).

This also brings to mind the assembly at Troas when Paul preached to midnight. Evidently this service lasted several hours as those present listened patiently. We are told that one of those in attendance fell asleep and fell out of a third story window (Acts 20:7-9).

The people in the assembly in the book of Nehemiah obviously meditated on the things that were read. Meditating on God's word brings blessings. "Blessed is the man who walks not in the counsel of the ungodly, nor stands in the path of sinners, nor sits in the seat of the scornful; but his delight is in the law of the LORD, and in His law he meditates day and night" (Psalm 1:1-2).

What about us? Do we worship in an unhurried manner? Do we daydream in the assembly about hobbies, work, what's for dinner? Do we meditate on spiritual things or material things? Do we hurriedly do our Bible lesson, hurriedly say our prayers at night, and hurriedly rush to services and back home? Are we in too big of a hurry to speak to our brothers and sisters in Christ, inquire as to their well-being, and seek to be of service to others? Do we hurry through life without paying attention to the spiritual aspect of life?

This Assembly Was Attentive To God's Word

The people in the assembly paid attention to the things being read—"and the ears of all the people [were attentive] to the Book of the Law" (Nehemiah 8:3).

Like those of Cornelius' household, they were anxious to hear the word of God. When Cornelius knew that Peter was coming to his house, he assembled friends and relatives to hear God's word. "...Now therefore, we are all present before God, to hear all the things commanded you by God" (Acts 10:33).

Not only do we need to be attentive to God's word, but the Bible teaches that we are to take heed to what we hear and how we hear. Then He said to them, "Take heed what you hear" (Mark 4:24) "Therefore take heed how you hear" (Luke 8:18).

One of the great stories in the Bible about listening to God is found in 1 Samuel, where God spoke to Samuel in the night. After Samuel heard the voice for the third time, he went to Eli and told him about it. Eli said, "Go, lie down; and it shall be, if He calls you, that you must say, 'Speak, LORD, for Your servant hears.'" So Samuel went and lay down in his place. Now the LORD came and stood and called as at other times, "Samuel! Samuel!" And Samuel answered, "Speak, for Your servant hears" (1 Samuel 3:9-10).

What about us? Do we listen to the word of God with an open mind? Do we listen to the right things? Do we pay attention during worship services? When the Lord speaks to us through His word, do we listen?

This Assembly Demonstrated Reverence

Nehemiah 8:5-6 shows the reverential attitude of the people. "And Ezra opened the book in the sight of all the people, for he was [standing] above all the people; and when he opened it, all the people stood up. And Ezra blessed the LORD, the great God. Then all the people answered, "Amen, Amen!" while lifting up their hands. And they bowed their heads and worshiped the LORD with [their] faces to the ground."

The bodily position says something about our reverence to God. In the three accounts of Jesus praying in Gethsemane, we are told that He prayed in three positions. We are told that Jesus knelt down (Luke 22:41), He fell on His face (Matthew 26:39), and He laid down on the ground (Mark 14:35). Certainly in this passage in Nehemiah, we can see that the people in attendance were reverent.

Habakkuk speaks of the reverence we should have for God: "But the LORD is in His holy temple. Let all the earth keep silence before Him" (Habakkuk 2:20).

The Hebrew writer points out that we are to serve God acceptably and with godly fear. "Therefore, since we are receiving a kingdom which cannot be shaken, let us have grace, by which we may serve God acceptably with reverence and godly fear" (Hebrews 12:28).

What about us? Are we reverent during worship services? I have witnessed from the pulpit, people talking, writing notes to each other, giggling, playing with a baby on the next pew or across the building. I have picked up a hand-full of gum and candy wrappers where several young people sat during the assembly. When I emptied my pocket of the trash in front of the church, I had one woman to "chew me out" and tell me her kids would not do such a thing. (Since she was not with them, she did not know what they would do. As a school principal, I dealt with parents all the time who told me that their children would not do such and such a thing, when I knew, and had evidence, that they were guilty.) Does this show reverence to God? I think not!

This Assembly Was Tenderhearted

The people were so touched in the assembly, they wept when they heard the words of the Law. "...This day [is] holy to the LORD your God; do not mourn nor weep." For all the people wept, when they heard the words of the Law" (Nehemiah 8:9).

Only those with a tender heart can have their hearts cut by the word of God. Those "cut to the heart" on Pentecost experienced a tenderness of heart. "Therefore let all the house of Israel know assuredly that God has made this Jesus, whom you crucified, both Lord and Christ." Now when they heard [this,] they were cut to the heart, and said to Peter and the rest of the apostles, "Men [and] brethren, what shall we do" (Acts 2:36-37)?

Christians need to be tenderhearted. If you were to take a large stone and try to stab it with a knife, what would happen? Obviously the knife would break and the stone would not be penetrated. The same is true spiritually. The "sword of the Spirit, which is the word of God" cannot penetrate a heart of stone (Ephesians 6:17). It must be tender and receptive in order to receive the gospel of Christ.

We must have tenderness and compassion one for another. Tenderness is seen upon Paul's departure to Jerusalem. "And when he had said these things, he knelt down and prayed with them all. Then they all wept freely, and fell on Paul's neck and kissed him, sorrowing most of all for the words which he spoke, that they would see his face no more. And they accompanied him to the ship" (Acts 20:36-38).

What about us? Does the word of God reach our hearts? Does

the story of the cross bring tears to our eyes? Do the stories of persecution of God's people break our hearts and give us strength?

This Assembly Was Willing To Change Their Ways

Their acceptance of the Law caused them to change. This is seen in verse 14-16 of Nehemiah chapter 8, when the people made booths to dwell in for seven days, a reminder of the time in which God made the children of Israel to dwell in booths when He brought them out of the land of Egypt (Leviticus 23:40-43). Nehemiah 8:17 tells us that they had not dwelt in booths since the days of Joshua, the son of Nun. This is a way of saying the people had not done this for a 1,000 years. Just because we have not done the things God requires of us for a long period of time does not mean that God has forgotten or that we should not return to what God has said. Skeptics tell us that Christianity is an old religion, 2,000 years old, and the Bible is out of place in our time. The truth of the matter is that God never changes and His word has not changed for 2,000 years, and a wise person would simply obey the word of God.

Living the Christian life requires change and Paul is an example of one who changed much when he accepted Christ. At one time, he had persecuted Christians and tried to destroy the church. Paul said he "persecuted the church of God beyond measure and [tried to] destroy it" (Galatians 1:13).

What about us? Are we willing to change? Do we blindly accept things taught because we were brought up in the church? Do we question the preacher? Do we search for truth?

This Assembly Found Joy In Worship

Ezra told them not to sorrow, and they had great gladness. "Go your way, eat the fat, drink the sweet, and send portions to those for whom nothing is prepared; for [this] day [is] holy to our LORD. Do not sorrow, for the joy of the LORD is your strength" (Nehemiah 8:10). Verse 17 says, "And there was very great gladness."

When one determines to obey Christ, we should be joyful. The Ethiopian man was joyful when he obeyed the gospel by being baptized: "So he commanded the chariot to stand still. And both Philip and the eunuch went down into the water, and he baptized him. Now when they came up out of the water, the Spirit of the Lord caught Philip away, so that the eunuch saw him no more; and he went on his way rejoicing" (Acts 8:38-39).

We are also told that the apostles had joy when they suffered for Christ. "And they agreed with him (Gamaliel-FR), and when they had called for the apostles and beaten [them,] they commanded that they should not speak in the name of Jesus, and let them go. So they departed from the presence of the council, rejoicing that they were counted worthy to suffer shame for His name (Acts 5:40-41).

What about us? The Bible tells us that we are to "Rejoice in the Lord always. Again I will say, rejoice" (Philippians 4:4)! Are we glad when we can come to worship God? David said, "I was glad when they said to me, 'Let us go into the house of the Lord.'" (Psalm 122:1). Do we find joy in coming to worship services? Do we find joy in serving others as God would have us to? Are we concerned about the needs of others? Do we count it a joyful thing to suffer for Christ?

The Sacred Assembly

Nehemiah tells us that following the seven days of assembling to read the Law of the Lord, there was a sacred assembly according to the prescribed manner. Nine times in the Bible we find mentioned sacred assemblies. The rare Hebrew word, translated sacred, means "restrain or confine," and is rendered "solemn assembly." Many assemblies today are not sacred, not restrained, nor confined to the pattern or according to the ordained way. They resemble a "pep rally" more than they do a "solemn assembly according to the prescribed manner."

Conclusion

What is your attitude toward the assembly? Do you find yourself to be unhurried, attentive, reverent, tenderhearted, willing to change, and finders of joy? The people in Nehemiah chapter eight had these things. I believe they are things we should find in our worship today. Paul said, "Examine yourselves [as to] whether you are in the faith. Test yourselves. Do you not know yourselves that Jesus Christ is in you–unless indeed you are disqualified" (2 Corinthians 13:5)?

Chapter 7

Emotionalism in Worship

We have all seen it on television and perhaps some have experienced it personally. The emotionally charged worship service begins. The carefully orchestrated high-tech modern worship service offers pablum from the pulpit and a circus for the soul. The show begins when the "praise leader" strikes up the band. The crowd rises from their seats. The praise leader exhorts by waving his arms in the air and the congregation follows. He is the cheerleader, exciting the crowd. Soon they are swaying with the music, waving their hands in the air. If the crowd is a little dull, he changes the key, increases the volume, and urges everyone to be happy in their worship experience. The experience is not unlike a pop music concert. There are flashing lights, large video screens, and loud music is magnified on high-powered audio equipment. There are performers to sing, choirs to harmonize, and liturgical dancers. Every performance receives an appreciative applause from the crowd.

The preacher, the "Reverend Doctor Smiley", walks to the pulpit. He is an extremely talented man. He knows the most important thing is how the people in the assembly feel. He strokes the collective ego and preaches a "feel good" message that is usually summed up in three words—**God Loves You!** The men give him the greatest of respect—he is a great spiritual man in their estimation. The women think he is awesome and the kids love his jokes, talent and leadership. But when the service is over, the sound system turned off, the guitars unplugged, and the keyboard covered, the serious student of God's word must ask, "Was all this for God's benefit or for man's benefit?" "Was this godly worship?"

In an article by Monte Wilson entitled "Narcissism Goes to Church," Wilson refers to this type of service as a Church-O-Rama. He says, "It is the exaltation of emotional gratification outside any theological parameters. We are in love with ourselves and evaluate churches, ministers and truth-claims based upon how they make us feel about ourselves." Wilson concludes his article by saying, "Those who have been attending Church-O-Rama who are truly seeking God, will discover that what they have been fed is cotton candy for the soul and all they have to show for years of eating such things is a heart and head filled with cavities." Indeed, religious sociologists say that they see a growing fixation on the modern worship experience rather than a fixation on godliness.

Is It Wrong To Show Emotion In Worship?

Absolutely not! God gave us emotions. Emotions are feelings, often intense, which can have an effect on the physical body. Emotion is a stirred up reaction, such as love (1 Peter 4:8), fear (Matthew 10:28), sorrow (2 Corinthians 7:10), joy (Philippians 4:4), etc. Can we separate these feelings from acceptable worship? Does God require that our service to Him be without emotion? Does God desire that we be "bored stiff"? Does God want us to sing without emotion or day-dream during the Lord's Supper? Does God require bland sermons and half-hearted efforts on the part of the preacher? Are there feelings that should be touched during worship?

Many times I have shed tears in worship. Sometimes they were tears of joy in seeing someone respond to the gospel invitation. Sometimes they were tears of sadness. Sometimes tears of grief as I thought of the burden of sin, or as I tried to visualize the suffering of the Lord. Often, I have been overjoyed in the song service as the beauty of the song touched my heart, knowing that we were singing praises to the Lord and edifying one another in song.

Notice that two emotions—love and joy, are listed as fruit of the Spirit in Galatians 5:22. Many times the scriptures use the words joy and rejoice. This is an emotion we must have. Paul tells us, "Finally, my brethren, rejoice in the Lord…" (Philippians 3:1). And again he says, "Rejoice in the Lord always. Again I will say, rejoice" (Philippians 4:4)! Singing often brings about emotions of joy. We are told to sing in Ephesians 5:19, where Paul says, "speaking to one another in psalms and hymns and spiritual songs, singing and making melody in your heart to the Lord…" In the Old Testament we read, "Be glad then, you children of Zion, and rejoice in the LORD your God" (Joel 2:23). The psalmist said, "I was glad when they said to me, 'Let us go into the house of the LORD.'" (Psalm 122:1). God wants His people to be glad, to rejoice, to be happy, and celebrate life. Emotion is a part of the life of every sincere servant of Christ.

Emotion Differs From Emotionalism

Emotionalism as related to worship is much different from emotion. Emotionalism is being guided by feeling rather than truth. It is the old "better felt than told" religion, where feelings trump logic and reasoning, and the feeling itself becomes the "evidence." When we abdicate truth on the altar of feeling, then our sacrifice is unacceptable to God. There are many examples in the Bible of people who made decisions based on feelings.

The Example of Eve- Even though God had commanded that Adam and Eve not eat of the tree in the midst of the garden, Satan deceived Eve into thinking that it was all right. Intellectually, Eve knew it was wrong, but her feelings, produced by a false revelation, caused her to eat the forbidden fruit. "So when the woman saw that the tree was good for food, that it was pleasant to the eyes, and a tree desirable to make one wise, she took of its fruit and ate. She also gave to her husband with her, and he ate" (Genesis 3:6). The emotions produced by feelings (lust of the flesh, eyes, and pride of life-1 John 2:15) caused her to follow her emotions rather than what she knew intellectually.

The Example of Jacob- One great example of the inaccuracy of feelings is found in the story of Joseph. Joseph's father, Jacob, believed that Joseph had been killed by a wild animal when his brothers brought Joseph's blood soaked coat to their father. The Bible says, "And he recognized it and said, 'It is my son's tunic. A wild beast has devoured him. Without doubt Joseph is torn to pieces.' Then Jacob tore his clothes, put sackcloth on his waist, and mourned for his son many days" (Genesis 37:33-34). Although Joseph was alive, for many years Jacob thought he was dead. Even though Joseph was alive and well, the pain and anguish that Jacob felt for his son was real. His emotion of grief was based on a false premise.

The Example of Demas- 2 Timothy 4:10 says **"Demas loved the present world..."** Love is an emotion. Intellectually, Demas knew the truth and what he should do. However, the emotion of love for the world overtook him.

The Example of Festus- "Now as he reasoned about righteousness, self-control, and the judgment to come, **Felix was afraid** and answered, "Go away for now; when I have a convenient time I will call for you" (Acts 24:25). Intellectually, Festus believed what Paul taught. Paul reasoned with him, using the power of knowledge. Paul spoke to the intellect of Festus. However, the emotion of fear that Felix had, overruled the knowledge that Paul presented to him.

The Example of Agrippa- (Acts 26:27-29) Paul knew that Agrippa believed the gospel but was unable to get him to act on his knowledge. Paul said, "I know that you do believe" (Acts 26:27).

Perhaps Agrippa, like Festus, was afraid. The emotion of fear (of losing his soul) could have served Agrippa well. Whether the fear was caused by the realization that he was lost, or what would happen to him if he accepted Christ, we do not know. Often times fear can keep us from doing what we know we ought to do. Such is the case in our next example.

The Example of the One Talent Man- In Matthew 25:14-30, Jesus shares with us the Parable of the Talents. In this parable, the one talent man was gripped with the emotion of fear. This fear kept him from doing what he should have done with the money entrusted to him. As a result of the emotion of fear, the man was lost. "And cast the unprofitable servant into the outer darkness. There will be weeping and gnashing of teeth" (Matthew 25:30). The Bible points out that many of the inhabitants of hell will be there because of the emotion of fear. "But **the fearful**, and unbelieving, and the abominable, and murderers, and whoremongers, and sorcerers, and idolaters, and all liars, shall have their part in the lake which burneth with fire and brimstone: which is the second death" (Revelation 21:8 KJV).

When emotionalism becomes our guide to worship, we are engaged in the idolatry of emotionalism. The emotion itself becomes our god. Feelings are fickle. Feelings can be affected by what we eat, by loud music or lighting, or any number of external stimuli. Several years ago a young man told me he accepted Mormonism because he prayed about it and when he did, he developed a strange feeling, like butterflies in his stomach. He felt that this was God's way of telling him he found the truth. A friend of mine told him, "I coach football, and I get that same feeling every Friday night before the game. That doesn't mean I'm having a religious experience."

Are We Converted By Emotionalism or Truth?

Exciting the emotions leaves much undone in the realm of logic and reasoning. In fact, this is contrary to the Bible. At Thessalonica, Paul "**reasoned** with them from the scriptures" (Acts 17:2); at Athens "he **reasoned** in the synagogue with the Jews and with the Gentile worshipers, and in the marketplace daily with those who happened to be there" (Acts 17:17); at Corinth "He **reasoned** in the synagogue every Sabbath, and persuaded both Jews and Greeks" (Acts 18:4); at Ephesus, "he went into the synagogue and spoke boldly for three months, **reasoning** and persuading concerning the things of the kingdom of God" (Acts 19:8), and he was also "**reasoning** daily in the school of Tyrannus" (Acts 19:9).

Jesus said it is the truth that "makes us free" (John 8:32). James says the implanted word "is able to save your souls" (James 1:21), and Peter says we are born again by the incorruptible seed, which is "the word of God which lives and abides forever" (1 Peter 1:23). Jesus said "He who rejects me and does not receive my words, has that which judges him—the word that I have spoken will judge him in the last day" (John 12:48). We are converted by accepting God's word and doing His will, not by some emotional experience or religious feeling!

Can you picture the apostle Paul preaching in some church today with a "rock concert" atmosphere? Can you see Paul trying to excite the crowd by using the techniques of today's preachers—techniques to arouse emotions that would cause people to forget the solemnity of worship to God, and devote himself to the exercise of a feel-good religion? God could have implemented any technique He wanted, but God chose the "foolishness of preaching" to save the souls of men. Paul said, "But we preach Christ crucified, to the Jews a stumbling block, and to the Greeks foolishness, but to those who are called, both Jews and Greeks, Christ the power of God and the wisdom of God. Because the foolishness of God is wiser than men, and the weakness of God is stronger than men" (1 Corinthians 1:23-25).

Emotionalism In Worship In The Nineteenth Century

Emotionalism in worship has been around for a long time. The "Great Awakening" of religious fervor was demonstrated in August 1801, when according to the estimate of Barton W. Stone, twenty to thirty thousand people showed up for a camp meeting at Cane Ridge, Kentucky. From Barton Stone's autobiography, Stone described the emotionalism that took place at Cane Ridge, and listed some of the "exercises" as he called them. Among these manifestations of extreme emotionalism were:

Falling down- where people would fall to the ground as though they were dead.

The jerks- The subject would be affected and *"jerk backward and forward, or from side to side, so quickly that the features of the face could not be distinguished."*

Dancing- This *"generally began with the jerks, and was peculiar to professors of religion." "The subject, after jerking awhile, began to dance, and then the jerks would cease."*

Barking exercise- Many times the one who had the jerks would often grunt or make a barking sound.

Laughing exercise- Stone said *"it was a loud, hearty laughter."*

Running exercise- Stone said that the running exercise *"was nothing more than, that persons feeling something of these bodily agitations, through fear, attempted to run away, and thus escape from them."*

Singing exercise- Stone says, *"The subject in a very happy state of mind would sing most melodiously, not from the mouth or nose, but entirely in the breast, the sounds issuing thence."*

While the logical mind has trouble explaining these "exercises", the emotional mind will quickly attribute such things to a direct operation of the Holy Spirit, ushering in a "Great Awakening" of religion in a spiritually starved western frontier. However, Stone concludes this story by saying, "There were many eccentricities, and much fanaticism in this excitement." Fanaticism is defined as "irrational zeal." Irrational is defined as the antithesis of the ability to reason, or of being of a sound mind.

One of the great preachers of the 19th century was B. F. Hall, who learned the truth after reading the Campbell-McCalla debate in the year 1826. Hall, in his unpublished autobiography, tells of the general and accepted preaching style of the early 19th century.

"The religion of those days consisted principally of feeling; and those who shouted the loudest and made the greatest ado, were looked upon as the best Christians. Hence our preaching, our prayers, and songs we adapted to excite the emotions. We would clap and rub our hands, stamp with our feet, slain down (sic) and tear up the Bible, speak as loud as possible and scream at the top of our voice, to get up an excitement. I often blistered my hands by clapping and rubbing them together; and my feet were made sore by repeated stamping... I was excitable, and dealt much in the pathetic."

By his own account, Hall states that the purpose of his preaching, and the preaching of others, was to excite the emotions of the listeners. This was accomplished by loud preaching, clapping the hands, stamping the feet, being slain down, and tearing up Bibles. Hall even admitted that his favorite subjects were those where he could play on people's emotions. "Here fancy had ample room for play," he stated. Hall said that he was the one people turned to when "excitement was desired." Hall said all of this was for the purpose of "getting religion" and "getting through", both expressions of the "Mourner's Bench" religion of the day, when one was believed to be saved through a "religious experience."

Conclusion

Emotionalism is a stark contrast to the logical, rational, reasoning of the New Testament (Acts 17:2, 17; 18:4; 19:8-9). When the validity of Christianity is based on emotionalism rather than knowledge of God's word, we find a system of religion in deep spiritual poverty. One writer said, "Emotion without truth produces empty frenzy and cultivates shallow people who refuse the discipline of rigorous thought."

Beware brethren! "We are warming by the devil's campfire."

Chapter 8

Women In Leadership Roles In Worship

As a former school administrator, I occasionally will go back to the school where I spent most of my adult life. Last year I was invited to attend a reception honoring a graduating class on their twentieth anniversary of graduation. A member of the graduating class came up to me and told me how glad she was to see me and said, "Mr. Richey, I've decided to follow in your footsteps." "Really", I replied, thinking that this woman had become a school administrator. Her next statement took me by surprise. "Yes, Mr. Richey, I've decided to be a preacher like you."

More and more women are "entering the ministry" these days, and doing so without a scrap of biblical authority. Lending credence to the women ministers are a host of well-knowns, with perhaps the most well-known being Jimmy Carter, former president of the United States, who broke with the Southern Baptist Convention. His reason for doing so was the group's positions, including barring women pastors and declaring that wives should "submit graciously" to their husbands, and "violate the basic premises of my Christian faith," Carter wrote. Carter said he came to this decision "with a great deal of pain and reluctance." He added, "I personally feel that the Bible says all people are equal in the eyes of God. I personally feel that women should play an absolutely equal role in service of Christ in the church."

Another famous Baptist, Tony Campolo, author of twenty-eight books; guest on various programs including Nightline, Crossfire, and CNN News; and a speaker in demand for high schools, universities, conferences and retreats all over the country, was reported in 2003 in the Baptist Press News, as saying, "Anyone who resists the notion of women preachers is functioning as a tool of the devil." "It's one thing to be wrong, but that isn't wrong, that's sinful", Campolo said about opposing women preachers. He went on to say, "'Neglect not the gift that is in you,' and when women are gifted with the gift of preaching, anybody who frustrates that gift is an instrument of the devil."

How Extensive Is Acceptance of Women Preachers?

Studies show exponential growth of women clergy in the fifteen largest Protestant denominations between 1977 and 1994 (according to Zikmund, Lummis, and Chang, published in their study, Clergy Women: An Uphill Calling). Citing a Hartford Seminary study during that period of time, the number of female clergy increased significantly. Notice the increase of women in the clergy for the following denominations: American Baptist Church—from 157 to 712; Episcopal Church USA—94 to 1,394; Disciples of Christ—388 to 988; Evangelical Lutheran Church in America—73 to 1,519; Presbyterian Church (USA)—350 to 2,705; and the United Methodist Church—319 to 3,003. Interesting also, was the statistic that 25 percent of the female clergy and 19 percent of the male clergy who participated in the study were divorced. The study concluded, "Clergy women are reinventing ministry for the future, refusing the old definitions and expectations. Clergy women are expanding the very essence of Christian ministry and guiding the whole church to rethink and renew its leadership and membership" (p. 153).

Another paper points out that the Assemblies of God have licensed and ordained 4,000 women; the Southern Baptist convention, which passed a resolution prohibiting women pastors has 1,225 ordained Southern Baptist women, with roughly 200 serving as pastors and associate pastors (Fall, 1997 edition of Folio, the newsletter of Baptist Women in Ministry). The United Methodist Church has ordained 4,743 women clergy since 1956; the Presbyterian Church has 2,419 female leaders and the Episcopal Church in the United States has 1,070 ordained women.

Arguments for Women Preachers

On the website of a denominational church, a list of reasons was given for having women preachers. Notice the reasons that were listed and the scriptures that refute that position.

There is not one scripture forbidding women from preaching. 1 Corinthians 14:34-35 and 1 Timothy 2:11-15 forbid women from speaking in the assembly. It is hard to preach without speaking!

God is no respecter of persons. Amen! That's what the Bible says. Acts 10:34 and Galatians 3:28 are verses offered as proof texts for accepting women preachers in worship services; and since God is no respecter of persons, then some conclude God allows women to preach. The context of Acts 10:34 which says, "Then Peter opened his mouth and said: "'In truth I perceive that God shows no partiality'" shows that there is no difference between Jews and Gentiles in the sight of God. Galatians 3:28 says, "There is neither Jew nor Greek, there is neither slave nor free, there is neither male nor female; for you are all one in Christ Jesus." This doesn't mean that Jews quit being Jews, Gentiles quit being Gentiles, women quit being women and that slaves are no longer slaves. These roles continue. The roles of masters and servants continue (1 Timothy 6:1-2), and the roles of women and men continue. Women are to still be silent in the church (1 Corinthians 14:34-35; 1 Timothy 2:11-15), and men are to still be the head of the wives and wives are to submit to their husbands and husbands are to be the head of the wife (Ephesians 5:22-23). We are all free in Christ—free from the eternal wages of sin—but not free from earthly positions and responsibilities that God has given us.

The Great Commission is a command for all to preach the gospel. True, but women are prohibited from speaking to the church. All can preach privately as Phillip did when he "preached Jesus" to the Ethiopian (Acts 8:35). This was one-on-one preaching. Priscilla, the wife of Aquila, assisted him in "preaching," i.e., explaining the way of God more accurately (Acts 18:26). This was done privately and not publicly in the assembly of the church.

It is an undeniable fact that God called and anointed thousands of women to preach the gospel. I challenge anyone to name just one. Out of all those thousands of examples of women preachers purportedly mentioned in the Bible, why wasn't one named? The article goes on to say, "When someone says, 'God does not call women to preach,' it is like saying that God does not baptize with the Holy Spirit today." Well, God does not baptize with the Holy Spirit today. Ephesians 4:5 says there is "one baptism." That baptism is water baptism for the remission of sins (Acts 2:38). If Holy Spirit baptism is still around, that makes two baptisms; and God, speaking through Paul, an inspired writer, would be wrong.

Women preachers are a fulfillment of Bible prophecy. Absolutely not! We are told women would prophesy. Peter in the first gospel sermon on the Day of Pentecost quoted from the Old Testament prophet, Joel. He said, "'And it shall come to pass in the last days, says God, That I will pour out of My Spirit on all flesh; Your sons and **your daughters shall prophesy**, Your young men shall see visions, Your old men shall dream dreams. And on My menservants and on My maidservants I will pour out My Spirit in those days; **And they shall prophesy**" (Acts 2:17-18). We are also told that Philip, the evangelist, had four daughters that prophesied

(Acts 21:8-9). Women obviously prophesied during the times of miracles in the first century church. But the statement that women preachers are a fulfillment of Bible prophecy is a fabrication of man and not a revelation of God!

Prophesying and preaching are different. They prophesied during the days of miracles when God used men and women to prophesy, but nothing is ever said about a woman preaching in the New Testament Church. The miraculous gifts of the first century have ceased, therefore women do not prophesy today. There are many false teachers that claim to prophesy. They disgrace Christianity by their false claims.

The Bible declares women will prophesy. I agree with this statement, and the scriptures mentioned above prove this to be true. But again, preaching and prophesying are two different things. We cannot find anywhere in scripture where even one woman preached a single sermon.

God used women preachers in the Old Testament. Please provide book, chapter, and verse to prove this point. The author of the article uses the example of Deborah, who judged Israel. She was not a preacher. He also uses Miriam, a prophetess, and Huldah, who was sought by five men for her counsel in a private setting and says she was a preacher. He mentions another prophetess, but nowhere is the scripture found that tells of a woman preacher in the Old Testament.

God used women preachers in the New Testament. Again, where is the book, chapter, and verse that proves God used women preachers? I know of no such authority. I have never seen the passage that tells of women preachers.

There is no sound reason why a woman should not preach the gospel. None at all EXCEPT that there is no biblical authority for women preachers. Please give book chapter, and verse.

1 Corinthians 14:34-35 does not say anything about women preachers. True. It just says women are to keep silent in the church. If women preachers are women, they are forbidden to speak. That eliminates women preachers.

1 Timothy 2:12 is not a blanket rule for all women of all churches. How can one deny that the book of 1 Timothy is a rule for all men and women of all ages? It is in perfect agreement with the Book of Genesis as to the roles of men and women. The book was written so we can know how to behave ourselves in God's church. Paul says, "but if I am delayed, I write so that you may know how you ought to conduct yourself in the house of God, which is the church of the living God, the pillar and ground of the truth" (1 Timothy 3:15). The proper way to conduct ourselves in God's church is for women to be silent (1 Corinthians 14:34-35, 1 Timothy 2:11-15).

Titus 1: 6-7 points out a difference between a preacher and a bishop. This is correct but the writer proves nothing by his point because he doesn't understand the words bishop and pastor. The assumption is made that "pastor" is a biblical term for a preacher. Although a preacher can be a pastor, a pastor is the same as a bishop or overseer. The three Greek words for office leadership in the church are "Presbuteros" (from which we get the words elder and presbyter), "Episcopos" (from which we get the words bishop and overseer), and "Poimen" (from which we get the words pastor and shepherd). All of these Greek words are used interchangeably in two places in the Bible—Acts 20:17 & 28 and 1 Peter 5:1-4. The term "pastor" never means preacher. A pastor is one who oversees the church. The denominational concept of a "pastor" is a preacher that is in charge of a church. This concept of church leadership is unknown in the scriptures.

To condemn women preachers is a serious offense. To allow women preachers is a serious offense against God and His holy word. It is absolutely presumptuous to allow women to preach. We have no authority for women preachers. Where is the precept, example or inference of a woman ever preaching in a New Testament church? It is not there and the book, chapter, and verse cannot be produced! We can, however, find where women are to keep silent in the church (1 Corinthians 14:34; 1 Timothy 2:11-15).

While the author used five pages to make his points, and the author applied, or rather misapplied, a number of scriptures, the space of this treatise will not allow full disclosure of his position. I believe this position has "twisted scripture to its own destruction" (2 Peter 3:16). To understand God's prescribed role for women, we must turn to the pages of holy writ.

Biblical View of Women's Role in The Local Church

Genesis 2:18- And the LORD God said, "It is not good that man should be alone; I will make him a helper (help meet-KJV) comparable to him."

Genesis 2:21-24- And the LORD God caused a deep sleep to fall on Adam, and he slept; and He took one of his ribs, and closed up the flesh in its place. Then the rib which the LORD God had taken from man He made into a woman, and He brought her to the man. And Adam said: "This is now bone of my bones and flesh of my flesh; She shall be called Woman, Because she was taken out of Man. Therefore a man shall leave his father and mother and be joined to his wife, and they shall become one flesh.
In these verses, at the beginning of man's existence in the Garden of Eden, God established a relationship and positions that are eternal in nature. God made man and woman. God designated

that man was to have **HEADSHIP** and the woman was to be a **HELP MEET**. Every time man plays around with God's holy and divine arrangement for men and women, God's law is violated, and man, though wise in his own thinking, seeks to destroy the eternal plan of God for man. When woman assumes the role of Headship, she is not functioning in her God given role of Help Meet. When man is not assuming his role of Headship, it is extremely difficult for woman to be a Help Meet. This was and is God's plan for man. Man is to have Headship in the home, with his wife and children, and in the church, which was purchased with the blood of Christ. How do we know this? Notice these scriptures:

1 Corinthians 14:34-35- Let your women keep silent in the churches, for they are not permitted to speak; but they are to be submissive, as the law also says. And if they want to learn something, let them ask their own husbands at home; for it is shameful for women to speak in church.

1 Timothy 2:11-15- Let a woman learn in silence with all submission. And I do not permit a woman to teach or to have authority over a man, but to be in silence. For Adam was formed first, then Eve. And Adam was not deceived, but the woman being deceived, fell into transgression. Nevertheless she will be saved in childbearing if they continue in faith, love, and holiness, with self-control.

It is obvious from these scriptures that women preachers are in violation of the will of God. Either these verses are applicable to us today or they are archaic and must be discarded from the Bible. When one comes to the latter conclusion, then any portion of Holy Scripture can be discarded if it doesn't "fit" one's preconceived idea or personal conviction.

How can a woman be a preacher, elder, or deacon in the church, when she is forbidden to teach or usurp authority over a man?

Women preachers openly disobey the will of God and exert their own will above God's will for their own purpose.

Conclusion

God's plan for women shows that God gives women great and awesome responsibilities. The thoughts that we have presented are not popular and do not bode well with many in the religious world today. However, if we are to follow the will of God, we must do God's things in God's way. He has revealed His will in the Holy Bible. We choose whether we will do things God's way or our way. If one has already decided what he or she wants to believe on this subject, and does not care what God says, then no argument from scripture will change that opinion and further investigation of God's word will not change that individual's judgment or belief.

Part 2

How We Worship

Introduction

Now that we have looked at several topics concerning worship, we now move on to a study of biblical teachings about the actual worship service. We need to keep in mind that God has prescribed how He wants to be worshiped and that worship is to be directed to God and is not for the purpose of pleasing men. This often causes conflicts for individuals and groups. Obviously God wants us to gain from the worship. When we worship, we feel closer to God. Worship provides a sense of not only fulfillment of duty, but pleasure in knowing that we are giving back to God our time, money, energy, adoration, and praise to the Creator of the Universe. The conflict comes when man wants more out of the service than he is giving to God. God is to be the focus, the center of our worship—not man.

In the following chapters, we will deal with the five items of worship of the New Testament Church. Its worship is simple. Authority is found in the Bible for singing, praying, preaching, giving of financial support to the church, and partaking of the

Lord's Supper as a memorial feast to Christ the King. Nothing else is authorized in the scriptures concerning the worship of the New Testament Church. If these things were practiced when the inspired apostles were on the earth, they must be items of acceptable worship for us today.

Explore with us the worship of the New Testament Church as presented in the Holy Bible, the inspired, God-breathed, God-directed scripture that will judge us on the Day of Judgment (Revelation 20:12, 15).

Chapter 9

How We Worship—Singing

In order to ascertain truth on any biblical subject, we must turn to the Bible to see what God has said about the matter. Today, most churches have instrumental music in their worship services. We do not. Are we right? Are they wrong? Most people in the world and in various denominations think this is a ridiculous question, simply assuming that since they like instrumental music, God must like it also. All of my life I have dealt with questions about this subject, but usually they are of this nature: "Why do you Church of Christ not have instrumental music?" However, I have not known many that really cared about a scriptural answer. They simply want to raise the subject in order to point out how narrow-minded we are and, basically, how ridiculous we are to the rest of the world.

The real concern should not be what someone else thinks, or what I think, but what God has to say about the matter. I do affirm the following **(1)** The Bible authorizes vocal music (specifically, singing) in worship; **(2)** There is nothing wrong with instrumental music outside of worship; and **(3)** Instrumental music in worship is sinful because it violates the authority of the scriptures and is presumptuous on the part of man.

Will you be open-minded and look at this discussion? First, let us look at all of the verses in the New Testament on the subject of music.

Sung

Matthew 26:30 And when they had sung a hymn, they went out to the Mount of Olives.

Mark 14:26 And when they had sung a hymn, they went out to the Mount of Olives.

Sing

Romans 15:9 and that the Gentiles might glorify God for *His* mercy, as it is written: "For this reason I will confess to You among the Gentiles, And sing to Your name."

1 Corinthians 14:15 What is *the conclusion* then? I will pray with the spirit, and I will also pray with the understanding. I will sing with the spirit, and I will also sing with the understanding.

Hebrews 2:12 saying: "I will declare Your name to My brethren; In the midst of the assembly I will sing praise to You."

James 5:13 Is anyone among you suffering? Let him pray. Is anyone cheerful? Let him sing psalms.

Revelation 15:3 They sing the song of Moses, the servant of God, and the song of the Lamb, saying: "Great and marvelous *are* Your works, Lord God Almighty! Just and true *are* Your ways, O King of the saints!

Acts 16:25 But at midnight Paul and Silas were praying and singing hymns to God, and the prisoners were listening to them.

Singing

Ephesians 5:19 speaking to one another in psalms and hymns and spiritual songs, singing and making melody in your heart to the Lord.

Colossians 3:16 Let the word of Christ dwell in you richly in all wisdom, teaching and admonishing one another in psalms and hymns and spiritual songs, singing with grace in your hearts to the Lord.

Song

Revelation 5:9 And they sang a new song, saying: "You are worthy to take the scroll, And to open its seals; for You were slain, And have redeemed us to God by Your blood Out of every tribe and tongue and people and nation,

Revelation 14:3 They sang as it were a new song before the throne, before the four living creatures, and the elders; and no one could learn that song except the hundred *and* forty-four thousand who were redeemed from the earth.

Revelation 15:3 They sing the song of Moses, the servant of God, and the song of the Lamb, saying: "Great and marvelous *are* Your works, Lord God Almighty! Just and true *are* Your ways, O King of the saints!

As you read these verses, do you see in any of them where instrumental music was used in worship services? The answer is no. Nowhere in the New Testament do we find instruments being used in the worship of God in the services of the church.

Do We Have Biblical Authority For Instrumental Music In Worship?

Authority is defined as "right, power, or jurisdiction." So when we ask the question, "Do we have scriptural authority," we are asking if God has given us the right, power or jurisdiction in the matter under consideration.

Certainly the Bible teaches that we must have authority for what we do. Peter said, "If anyone speaks, let him speak as the oracles of God..." (1 Peter 4:11). Jesus asked, "But why do you call Me 'Lord, Lord,' and not do the things which I say" (Luke 6:46). This implies that we must do what Jesus says and that we must have authority for what we do. The apostle Paul said, "And whatever you do in word or deed, do all in the name of the Lord Jesus, giving thanks to God the Father through Him" (Colossians 3:17). To do all that is in the name of the Lord Jesus is to do those things for which we have biblical authority.

The Bible also teaches that we are not to go beyond those things written in God's word. "...that you might learn in us not to think of men above that which is written..." (1 Corinthians 4:6). To do so is a violation of authority.

Jesus settled the matter of instrumental music in worship when he left instrumental music out of the worship service of the church. The New Testament is silent concerning instrumental music in the worship. It is evident that those who have it in the worship do so without scriptural authority. We should not presume to add to the divine pattern. We must respect the silence of the scriptures. To speak where God has not spoken is to speak for God. Man assumes God agrees with his decision to do something, even though God has not given His permission. The Bible calls this the sin of presumption. David said, "Keep back Your servant also from presumptuous sins; Let them not have dominion over me. Then I shall be blameless, and I shall be innocent of great transgression" (Psalm 19:13). God said, "Now the man who acts presumptuously and will not heed the priest who stands to minister there before the LORD your God, or the judge, that man shall die. So you shall put away the evil from Israel" (Deuteronomy 17:12).

Is Instrumental Music In Worship From Man Or God?

When Jesus was confronted by the chief priest and elders as to where He received His authority, Jesus asked them, "The baptism of John, where was it from, from heaven or from men" (Matthew 21:25)? When they refused to answer, Jesus refused to give them His authority. Since we cannot find any biblical authority for instrumental music in the worship of the New Testament church, and since God did not authorize it, we must conclude that instrumental music came from man and not from God. This should be painfully obvious to proponents of instrumental music in light of the history of instrumental music in worship. Notice the following quotes about instrumental music from history:

"Pope Vitalian is related to have first introduced organs into some of the churches of Western Europe, about 670; but the earliest trustworthy account is that of the one sent as a present by the Greek emperor Constantine Copronymus to Pepin, King of the Francs, in 755" (The American Encyclopedia, Vol. 12, p. 688).

"In the Greek church, the organ never came into use. But after the eighth century, it became more and more common in the Latin Church; not, however, without opposition from the side of the monks. Its misuse, however, raised so great an opposition to it, that, but for the Emperor Ferdinand, it would probably have been abolished by the Council of Trent. The Reformed church discarded it; and though the Church of Basel very early re-introduced it, it was in other places admitted only sparingly, and after long hesitation" (The Schaff-Herzog Encyclopedia, Vol. 2, page 1702).

It is a matter of historic record that the apostolic church did not use mechanical instrumental music. Theodoret, Bishop of Cyrus in

Syria (ca. 393-460 AD), said, *"Simply singing is not agreeable to children, but singing with lifeless instruments and with dancing and clapping; on which account the use of this kind of instruments and of others agreeable to children is removed from the songs in the churches, and there is left remaining simply singing"* (Everett Furgeson's Acappella Music, quoting from Theodoret, Bishop of Cyrus), Question 107, p. 464).

The testimony of many others, especially those considered to be leaders or founders of denominations, is of importance in this discussion. Notice the following:

Martin Luther (founder of the Lutheran church): *"The organ in the worship of God is an ensign of Baal"* (McClintock & Strong Encyclopedia, Music, Vol. VI, p. 762).

John Calvin (founder of Presbyterianism): *"Musical instruments in celebrating the praises of God would be no more suitable than the burning of incense, the lighting of lamps, and the restoration of other shadows of the law"* (John Calvin's Commentary on the Twenty-third Psalm).

John Wesley (founder of Methodism): *"I have no objection to instruments of music in our chapels, providing they are neither heard nor seen"* (Clarke's Commentary, Vol. IV, p. 686).

Adam Clarke (Methodist, and one of the world's best-known Bible commentators): *"I am an old man and an old minister, and I here declare that I never knew instrumental music to be productive of any good in the worship of God; and have reason to believe it has been productive of much evil. Music, as a science, I esteem and admire, but instruments of music in the house of God I abominate and abhor. This is the abuse of music; and here I register my protest against all corruptions in the worship of the Author of Christianity"* (Clarke's Commentary, Vol. IV, p. 686).

Charles Spurgeon (one of the greatest preachers the Baptist church has ever produced, and for 20 years preached to 10,000 people every Sunday at the Metropolitan Baptist Tabernacle, London, England), when asked why he did not use the organ in worship, he quoted 1 Corinthians 14:15, and added, *"I would as soon pray to God with machinery as to sing to God with machinery"* (Instrumental Music In The Worship, M.C. Kurfees, p. 196).

Conybeare and Howson, famous scholars of the Church of England, in their commentary on Ephesians 5:19, said *"Make melody with the music of your hearts, to the Lord...let your songs be, not the drinking songs of heathen feasts, but psalms and hymns; and their accompaniment, not the music of the lyre, but the melody of the heart"* (Life and Epistles of St. Paul, Vol. II, p. 408).

The "Psallo" Argument

The argument is made that the Greek word **"psallo"** means to play an instrument. The word "psallo" is found *five times* in the New Testament; *three times it is translated "sing"; one time as "sing songs", and one time as "make melody".*

Isn't it interesting that forty-seven of the best Greek scholars in the world translated the word, "psallo" in the King James Version as sing, sing songs, and make melody, with nothing being said about playing an instrument. One hundred one of the best Greek scholars in the world translated the American Standard Version and they never rendered the word "psallo" play; rather, sing and make melody. W. E. Vine in his Expository Dictionary of New Testament Words says that the word "psallo", in New Testament times, meant to sing and make melody. James Strong, in his Dictionary of Greek Words, also says that the word, **"psallo"** in New Testament times meant to sing and make melody.

Notice that **(1)** the greatest scholars in the world agree that "psallo" meant sing. **(2)** Nowhere in the Bible is the word "psallo", rendered "play" **(3)** If "psallo" means play, then everyone must play

82

an instrument or violate the command of God. Every person attempting to worship God without an instrument is in rebellion to God's command.

Other Arguments Considered

People should use their talents to worship God. Some have the talent to dance, some to juggle, and some to yodel. Should they be given an opportunity to exercise these talents in worship services? What about calf roping, weight lifting, comic routines, and painting. I once knew a man that was the greatest I ever saw when it came to cleaning fish. Should he demonstrate his talent in worship services?

You have a piano in your home. If you can have one in your home, why can't you have one in the church? We have pets in our homes. Does this mean we should have pets in the church building? We have food in our homes. Does this mean we should eat in the church building? "What! Do you not have houses to eat and drink in? Or do you despise the church of God and shame those who have nothing? What shall I say to you? Shall I praise you in this? I do not praise you" (1 Corinthians 11:22).

The Bible talks of instruments in heaven. If so, why can't we have them in worship services on earth? This is clearly a reference to **Revelation 14:2**. While the **KJV** renders the passage, " I heard the voice of harpers harping with their harps:", the **ASV**, the **RSV**, the **CON** and the **NIV** all render this passage using *"like"* or *"as"* a harpist playing a harp.

If I said, "The backfire of the automobile was as the blast of a shotgun," this would not mean that the backfire was the blast of the shotgun! But even if there are harps in heaven, it is because God wills it. However, if God willed it in the worship of the Church, He forgot to mention it. I don't believe God is forgetful to tell us how He wants to be worshiped.

They had musical instruments in Old Testament worship. Yes, they did. But do you live under the Old Testament or the New Testament? Many know so little about the Bible; they don't understand the relationship of the Old and New Testaments. We as children of God live under the New Testament. The Old was taken out of the way and "nailed to the cross" (Colossians 2:14). They also burned incense under the Old Testament. The males went to Jerusalem every year (Ex: 23:17). The blood of bulls and goats was offered to God. Should we still keep the Old Law? Should we all go to Jerusalem each year and offer the blood of bulls and goats today?

God didn't say not to use instruments. Neither does the Bible say, "Thou shalt not baptize in oil,", "Thou shalt not baptize a baby,", "Thou shalt not sprinkle,", "Thou shalt not use ice cream and cake on the Lord's table." This is a ridiculous argument. If we presume that God doesn't mind, or that God doesn't care, we speak where God has not spoken. We speak for God, and we dare God to do anything about it. Presumption is a sin. "Keep back Your servant also from presumptuous *sins;* Let them not have dominion over me. Then I shall be blameless, And I shall be innocent of great transgression (Psalm 19:13).

Instruments are just aids, like song books, lights, pitch pipes, etc. It is not an aid; it is an addition. In fact, it changes "singing" into another kind of music. No longer do we have only vocal music (singing), we have instrumental music (playing). God said sing, **NOT** play. If you don't think that God is picky about how we worship, look at Leviticus 10 where God burnt the sons of Aaron to a crisp because they lit a sacrifice with fire which God had not commanded them. Or, look in Numbers 20, where God took the life of Aaron and refused to let Moses enter the Promised Land because God told them to speak to a rock so that water would come forth, and instead, Moses hit the rock with a stick. God says what He wants, and that eliminates everything else.

Conclusion

Since we have no biblical authority to have instrumental music in our worship—since no authority for this is found in the New Testament, we would be presumptuous to include such in our worship today. We need to "speak as the Bible speaks, and be silent where the Bible is silent" on these matters of worship.

We must ask ourselves if instrumental music in worship came from God or from man. Since God did not mention it as a part of the New Testament worship, and since it was not used in the churches for 600 years, it is obvious that instrumental music in worship is from man and not from God. Are you willing to risk your soul for something man dreamed up for worship? Think about it!

Chapter 10

How We Worship—Prayer, Part 1

The concept of prayer differs just as people differ. For some, the concept of prayer is "like a Visa card." Just run it through (or by God) and you can have anything you want. Others have the "fire department" concept of God. That is, when there is an emergency in your life, you call on Him. Still others have the view that God will perform miracles for them to bring about the request of the prayer.

I believe that God answers prayers today. But there is much we need to learn about the subject of prayer. In this lesson on prayer presented in two parts, we want to develop a better understanding of the subject of prayer from a biblical, rather than an emotional, perspective.

Since this lesson is part of a series of lessons on "How We Worship," we certainly want to emphasize that prayer was an important part of worship in the New Testament church. And since prayer is a much neglected subject, we want to try to understand the subject better.

The disciples of Jesus recognized the importance of prayer. The scriptures never mention them asking Jesus to teach them how to preach, but they did ask Him to teach them to pray. The Bible says, "Now it came to pass, as He was praying in a certain place, when He ceased, that one of His disciples said to Him, "Lord, teach us to pray, as John also taught his disciples" (Luke 11:1). Jesus answered the disciples by giving them a prayer model. So He said to them, "When you pray, say: 'Our Father in heaven, Hallowed be Your name. Your kingdom come, Your will be done on earth as [it is] in heaven. Give us day by day our daily bread. And forgive us our sins, for we also forgive everyone who is indebted to us. And do not lead us into temptation, but deliver us from the evil one'" (Luke 11:2-4).

Perhaps their interest in learning to pray was heightened by observing Jesus pray. Indeed, Jesus was a man of prayer. It seems that Jesus was constantly praying, many times slipping away privately to spend time talking to His Heavenly Father. Some of the times we see Jesus praying are: Following his baptism (Luke 3:21); before selecting the twelve (Luke 6:12); before His arrest (John 17:20-21); and while on the cross (Luke 23:34). Other times of prayer were when Jesus simply wanted to be alone in a quiet place to pray. In fact, we are told He looked for a quiet place to pray (Matthew 14:23 and Mark 1:35). He often withdrew Himself to pray (Luke 5:16; Luke 9:18). It seems that Jesus loved to be alone in prayer.

Jesus taught his disciples that God wants to answer our prayers. Notice this passage: "So I say to you, ask, and it will be given to you; seek, and you will find; knock, and it will be opened to you. "For everyone who asks receives, and he who seeks finds, and to him who knocks it will be opened. "If a son asks for bread from any father among you, will he give him a stone? Or if [he asks] for a fish, will he give him a serpent instead of a fish? "Or if he asks for an egg, will he offer him a scorpion? "If you then, being evil, know how to give good gifts to your children, how much more will [your] heavenly Father give the Holy Spirit to those who ask Him" (Luke 11:9-13)!

The New Testament Church Prayed

Since the purpose of this chapter is to point out that prayer was a part of worship in the New Testament church, we need to move on to that point. One verse showing this would establish biblical authority. However, there are many examples in the Bible of the New Testament church engaging in prayer.

The Church at Jerusalem prayed. The 3,000 added to the church on the day of Pentecost continued steadfastly in prayer. Luke writes, "Then those who gladly received his word were baptized; and that day about three thousand souls were added [to them.] And they continued steadfastly in the apostles' doctrine and fellowship, in the breaking of bread, and in prayers" (Acts 2:41-42).

The assembly in Acts 4 prayed. When the church was assembled, prayer was offered to God. "And when they had prayed, the place where they were assembled together was shaken; and they were all filled with the Holy Spirit, and they spoke the word of God with boldness" (Acts 4:31). This prayer is recorded for us in Acts 4:24-31.

When Peter was in prison, the church prayed for him. Peter had been arrested and the saints feared that he, like James, would be put to death. The church that met in the house of Mary prayed for Peter's release from prison (Acts 12:12). The Bible says, "Peter was therefore kept in prison, but **constant prayer was offered to God for him by the church**" (Acts 12:5).

The church prayed when selecting elders. Luke records this for us. "So when they had appointed elders in every church, and prayed with fasting, they commended them to the Lord in whom they had believed" (Acts 14:23).

The church at Corinth prayed for Paul. "You also helping together in prayer for us, that thanks may be given by many persons on our behalf for the gift granted to us through many" (2 Corinthians 1:11).

Paul concluded his speech to the Ephesians with prayer. "And when he had said these things, he knelt down and prayed with them all" (Acts 20:36).

The disciples prayed in the assembly at Philippi. "And on the Sabbath day we went out of the city to the riverside, where prayer was customarily made; and we sat down and spoke to the women who met there" (Acts 16:13). Notice also that this verse points out that it was their custom to pray.

Paul told the Colossian church to continue in prayer and asked the church to pray for him. "Continue earnestly in prayer, being vigilant in it with thanksgiving; meanwhile praying also for us, that God would open to us a door for the word, to speak the mystery of Christ, for which I am also in chains" (Colossians 4:2-3).

Paul asked the church in Thessalonica to pray for him. He simply says to the brethren, "Brethren, pray for us" (1 Thessalonians 5:25). Paul also instructed the church on their frequency of prayer by saying, "Pray without ceasing" (1 Thessalonians 5:17).

The disciples meeting at Tyre kneeled down on the shore and prayed. As they said farewell to Paul, Luke says, "We departed and went on our way; and they all accompanied us, with wives and children, till [we were] out of the city. And we knelt down on the shore and prayed" (Acts 21:5).

Surely from these examples, we can see that the New Testament church was a praying church. The apostle Paul said, "Imitate me as I also imitate Christ" (1 Corinthians 11:1). If we do that, we will be given over to prayer, just like Jesus. We will seek opportunities to talk to our Heavenly Father!

For What Should We Pray?

Now that we have established biblical authority for prayer in the assembly, and have seen by the example of Jesus that prayer is also to be private, the question arises, "For what should I pray?" Well, let's look at some biblical examples of things for which we are to pray. We begin by looking at the example prayer that Jesus gave to his disciples: "In this manner, therefore, pray: Our Father in heaven, Hallowed be Your name. Your kingdom come. Your will be done on earth as it is in heaven. Give us this day our daily bread. And forgive us our debts, as we forgive our debtors. And do not lead us into temptation, but deliver us from the evil one. For Yours is the kingdom and the power and the glory forever. Amen" (Matthew 6:9-13).

In this prayer, we find praise of God; thankfulness for food; forgiveness of sins; not to be led into temptation; and that we will be delivered from Satan. Notice the prayer begins and ends with praise to God. But let us now look at some other things for which we should pray.

We are to pray for our enemies. "But I say to you, love your enemies, bless those who curse you, do good to those who hate you, and pray for those who spitefully use you and persecute you" (Matthew 5:44).

We are to pray for laborers in the gospel. "Then He said to His disciples, "The harvest truly is plentiful, but the laborers are few. Therefore pray the Lord of the harvest to send out laborers into His harvest" (Matthew 9:37-38).

We are to pray for safety. Jesus in predicting the fall of Jerusalem said, "And pray that your flight may not be in winter or on the Sabbath" (Matthew 24:20).

We are to pray in times of temptation and before temptation. "Watch and pray, lest you enter into temptation. The spirit indeed is willing, but the flesh is weak" (Matthew 26:41).

We are to pray in times of difficulty. "Again, a second time, He went away and prayed, saying, "O My Father, if this cup cannot pass away from Me unless I drink it, Your will be done" (Matthew 26:42). "So He left them, went away again, and prayed the third time, saying the same words" (Matthew 26:44).

We are to pray that our faith will not fail. "And the Lord said, "Simon, Simon! Indeed, Satan has asked for you, that he may sift you as wheat. But I have prayed for you, that your faith should not fail; and when you have returned to Me, strengthen your brethren" (Luke 22:31-32).

We are to pray in times of decision. "And they proposed two: Joseph called Barsabas, who was surnamed Justus, and Matthias. And they prayed and said, 'You, O Lord, who know the hearts of all, show which of these two You have chosen'" (Acts 1:23-24).

We are to pray for forgiveness. "Repent therefore of this your wickedness, and pray God if perhaps the thought of your heart may be forgiven you" (Acts 8:22). "Then Simon answered and said, "Pray to the Lord for me, that none of the things which you have spoken may come upon me" (Acts 8:24).

We are to pray in times of illness. "Is anyone among you suffering? Let him pray. Is anyone cheerful? Let him sing psalms. Is anyone among you sick? Let him call for the elders of the church, and let them pray over him, anointing him with oil in the name of the Lord. And the prayer of faith will save the sick, and the Lord will raise him up. And if he has committed sins, he will be forgiven" (James 5:13-15).

We are to pray that love might continue. "And this I pray, that your love may abound still more and more in knowledge and all discernment, that you may approve the things that are excellent, that you may be sincere and without offense till the day of Christ, being filled with the fruits of righteousness which are by Jesus Christ, to the glory and praise of God" (Philippians 1:9-11).

We are to pray for the spreading of the gospel. "Continue earnestly in prayer, being vigilant in it with thanksgiving; meanwhile praying also for us, that God would open to us a door for the word, to speak the mystery of Christ, for which I am also in chains" (Colossians 4:2-3).

We are to pray for wisdom. "If any of you lacks wisdom, let him ask of God, who gives to all liberally and without reproach, and it will be given to him. But let him ask in faith, with no doubting, for he who doubts is like a wave of the sea driven and tossed by the wind. For let not that man suppose that he will receive anything from the Lord; he is a double-minded man, unstable in all his ways" (James 1:5-8).

We are to pray for all men. "Therefore I exhort first of all that supplications, prayers, intercessions, *and* giving of thanks be made *for all men*, for kings and all who are in authority, that we may lead a quiet and peaceable life in all godliness and reverence. For this *is* good and acceptable in the sight of God our Savior" (1 Timothy 2:1-3).

And, when we don't know how or what to pray for, we have help (intercession) from the Holy Spirit. "Likewise the Spirit also helps in our weaknesses. For we do not know what we should pray for as we ought, but the Spirit Himself makes intercession for us with groanings which cannot be uttered" (Romans 8:26). The word intercession means, "to make petition; plead with; seeking the presence and hearing of God on behalf of others." (W. E. Vine, Expository Dictionary of New Testament Words, p. 267.

How Should We Pray?

This was a question that the disciples asked Jesus (Luke 11:1). A part of the answer to that question was stated in Matthew's account, where Jesus mentions how not to pray. Jesus warned about praying hypocritically—standing in the synagogues or busy street corners so they could be seen by others. Jesus pointed out the importance of private prayers, even as He said, "Go into your room, and when you have shut your door, pray to your Father...". Jesus was also aware of those of His day who used repeated phrases. Jesus called them "vain repetitions" and told them not to use them. All of these points are made by Jesus in Matthew 6:5-7. Please take the time to read these verses.

Notice now some biblical suggestions as to how we are to pray.

We are to pray persistently. In the parable found in Luke 18:1-6, Jesus "spoke a parable to them, that men always ought to pray and not lose heart, saying: "There was in a certain city a judge who did not fear God nor regard man. Now there was a widow in that city; and she came to him, saying, 'Get justice for me from my adversary.' And he would not for a while; but afterward he said within himself, 'Though I do not fear God nor regard man, yet because this widow troubles me I will avenge her, lest by her continual coming she weary me.'" Then the Lord said, 'Hear what the unjust judge said.'" Sometimes people offer up a prayer and forget it. It may be that God is interested in hearing from us again (and perhaps again), so we might express our desire for a particular answer from God.

We are to pray humbly. In Luke 18:10-14, we have the story by Jesus of two men praying. Jesus points out that the prayer of the humble man was accepted, but the prayer of the one who was arrogant, self-righteous, and intent on telling God how good he was, was not accepted. Even though the self-righteous Pharisee was a very religious man (giving tithes and fasting twice each week), his attitude was all wrong. He was condescending toward the humble tax collector, thanking God that he was not like that man. Jesus said that the Pharisee was not justified before God.

We are to pray believing God will answer our prayers. Jesus said, "And whatever things you ask in prayer, believing, you will receive" (Matthew 21:22). And James said, "But let him ask in faith, with no doubting, for he who doubts is like a wave of the sea driven and tossed by the wind. For let not that man suppose that he will receive anything from the Lord; he is a double-minded man, unstable in all his ways" (James 1:6-8).

We are to pray according to God's will. Jesus prayed "Your will be done" (Matthew 26:42). So often when we pray, we want our will to be done, not God's will. John points out that we are to pray according to God's will. He said, "Now this is the confidence that we have in Him, that if we ask anything according to His will, He hears us" (1 John 5:14). God wants us to have blessings and He wants us to ask for them. This is seen in Matthew 7:7-11, where Jesus tells us to ask of God; and just as a father gives good gifts to his children, our heavenly Father wants to give good gifts to us. Oftentimes we ask for things and do not receive them. James tells us why. He says, "You ask and do not receive, because you ask amiss, that you may spend it on your pleasures" (James 4:3).

We are to pray with confidence and assurance. The Hebrew writer says, "Let us therefore come boldly to the throne of grace, that we may obtain mercy and find grace to help in time of need" (Hebrews 4:16). This doesn't mean that we are to come brashly, demanding that God answer our prayers. It means that we are to have confidence and assurance in our prayers and God's ability to answer them. The Revised Standard Version says, "Let us then with confidence draw near to the throne of grace".

Conclusion

Prayer should be an important part of the life of every Christian. To examine one's prayer life is to examine one's spiritual health. As one takes his temperature to determine if he has a fever, we can take our spiritual temperature by checking our prayer life. Do you pray often? Daily? Two or three times a day? Or, do you seldom find a quiet place and talk to God? This is one of the great blessings of being a Christian. Do we use it, or abuse it by failing to pray? We need to imitate Christ by praying often.

Chapter 11

How We Worship—Prayer, Part 2

In our last chapter, we introduced the subject of prayer. We emphasized that prayer was a part of the worship of the New Testament church, citing the examples of churches in Jerusalem, Corinth, Ephesus, Philippi, Thessalonica, and Tyre as scriptural authority for prayer as a part of worship by the church. We also considered the subject "For What Should We Pray?" We then considered "How We Should Pray." These points are not only of interest, but necessary in understanding the subject of prayer from a biblical perspective. Certainly, we want our prayers to be acceptable to God, so we will begin with that thought.

The way we communicate with God is through prayer. Ask yourself how well you are communicating with your Heavenly Father.

Are All Prayers Acceptable To God?

The Bible teaches that there are conditions of acceptable prayer. Keep in mind that even if we meet these conditions, God may not answer our prayer the way we want it answered. Someone has said that God answers prayers three ways: **(1)** Yes. **(2)** No, and **(3)** Maybe later, or not right now.

We are to be righteous. "For the eyes of the LORD [are] on the righteous, and His ears [are open] to their prayers; but the face of the LORD [is] against those who do evil" (1 Peter 3:12).

We are to keep God's commandments. "And whatever we ask we receive from Him, because we keep His commandments and do those things that are pleasing in His sight" (1 John 3:22). The Holy Spirit places the condition of commandment keeping and being pleasing to God as conditions for receiving blessings from God.

We are to pray in faith. "But let him ask in faith, with no doubting, for he who doubts is like a wave of the sea driven and tossed by the wind. For let not that man suppose that he will receive anything from the Lord" (James 1:6-7).

We are to pray in Jesus' name. "And [whatever] you do in word or deed, [do] all in the name of the Lord Jesus, giving thanks to God the Father through Him" (Colossians 3:17).

We are to pray with a forgiving spirit. "For if you forgive men their trespasses, your heavenly Father will also forgive you. But if you do not forgive men their trespasses, neither will your Father forgive your trespasses" (Matthew 6:14-15).

We are to pray with the right motive in mind. "You ask and do not receive, because you ask amiss, that you may spend [it] on your pleasures" (James 4:3).

We must not abuse prayer. Men abuse prayer by thinking prayer is all that is necessary to please God. In fact, most protestant denominations teach that we are saved by prayer. How often I've heard, "Just accept Christ as your personal Savior, and pray the sinner's prayer." The problem with this is that nowhere in the Bible can one find the passage that teaches that an alien sinner is saved by prayer!

We can also abuse prayer by praying to be seen of men. Jesus warns about hypocritical prayer when He said, "And when you pray, you shall not be like the hypocrites. For they love to pray standing in the synagogues and on the corners of the streets, that they may be seen by men. Assuredly, I say to you, they have their reward. "But you, when you pray, go into your room, and when you have shut your door, pray to your Father who [is] in the secret [place;] and your Father who sees in secret will reward you openly. "And when you pray, do not use vain repetitions as the heathen [do.] For they think that they will be heard for their many words. "Therefore do not be like them. For your Father knows the things you have need of before you ask Him" (Matthew 6:5-8).

Our prayers should be without hypocrisy. As mentioned in the previous passage; Jesus condemned those who stood in the synagogues and street corners, praying to be heard of men. Jesus points out that their reward is that others see them pray. This obviously means God does not answer their prayers.

We are to pray without ceasing. "Pray without ceasing, in everything give thanks; for this is the will of God in Christ Jesus for you" (1 Thessalonians 5:17-18). This simply means that we are to be constant and consistent in prayer. It also teaches that we are to give thanks to God. How often do we pray for things and then fail to thank God for the blessing we receive?

We are to pray without wavering. "If any of you lacks wisdom, let him ask of God, who gives to all liberally and without reproach, and it will be given to him. But let him ask in faith, with no doubting, for he who doubts is like a wave of the sea driven and tossed by the wind. For let not that man suppose that he will receive anything from the Lord; [he is] a double-minded man, unstable in all his ways" (James 1:5-8). A lack of faith is a "prayer killer" if there ever was one.

We are not to be self-righteous. Such was the Pharisee in the account of Luke. "Two men went up to the temple to pray, one a Pharisee and the other a tax collector. "The Pharisee stood and prayed thus with himself, 'God, I thank You that I am not like other men, extortioners, unjust, adulterers, or even as this tax collector. 'I fast twice a week; I give tithes of all that I possess.' "And the tax collector, standing afar off, would not so much as raise [his] eyes to heaven, but beat his breast, saying, 'God, be merciful to me a sinner!' "I tell you, this man went down to his house justified [rather] than the other; for everyone who exalts himself will be humbled, and he who humbles himself will be exalted" (Luke 18:10-14).

We are not to use vain repetitions. Jesus said, "And when you pray, do not use vain repetitions as the heathen [do.] For they think that they will be heard for their many words" (Matthew 6:7). The Revised Standard Version says, "And in praying do not heap up empty phrases as the Gentiles do; for they think that they will be heard for their many words." Albert Barnes says of this passage that vain repetitions *"means to repeat a thing often, to say the same thing in different words, or to repeat the same words, as though God did not hear at first."*

Types of Prayers

There are several ways that people list the types of prayers that we are to offer to God. However, I find the following mnemonic device (memory device) to be helpful. The acronym, **A-C-T-S**, serves as an aid to our memory as we pray. Each letter stands for a word. Notice the following: **A – Adoration; C – Confession; T – Thanksgiving; S – Supplication.** Let's look at each of these words.

A- Adoration- Prayer is a time to adore and praise God. We should not just ask things of God. We should also acknowledge His awesomeness. How seldom do our prayers focus on God rather than what we want or need? 1 Chronicles 29:11 says, "Yours, O LORD, is the greatness, The power and the glory, The victory and the majesty; For all that is in heaven and in earth is Yours; Yours is the kingdom, O LORD, And You are exalted as head over all."

Consider the throne scene in the book of Revelation: "The four living creatures, each having six wings, were full of eyes around and within. And they do not rest day or night, saying: "Holy, holy, holy, Lord God Almighty, Who was and is and is to come" (Revelation 4:8). "You are worthy, O Lord, to receive glory and honor and power; for You created all things, and by Your will they exist and were created" (Revelation 4:11). "And they sang a new song, saying: "You are worthy to take the scroll, And to open its seals; For You were slain, And have redeemed us to God by Your blood Out of every tribe and tongue and people and nation, And have made us kings and priests to our God; And we shall reign on the earth" (Revelation 5:9-10). "And every creature which is in heaven and on the earth and under the earth and such as are in the sea, and all that are in them, I heard saying: "Blessing and honor and glory and power Be to Him who sits on the throne, And to the Lamb, forever and ever" (Revelation 5:13). Surely these passages show us the importance of honoring the Holy God Almighty!

C- Confession- Prayer is also a time to confess sin. One whose iniquities have separated him from God should exercise this privilege. Admit your wrongs! John said, "If we confess our sins, He is faithful and just to forgive us *our* sins and to cleanse us from all unrighteousness" (1 John 1:9).

T- Thanksgiving- In prayer, we should express our gratitude to God. It is "with thanksgiving" that our requests are to be made known to Him. Paul said, "Be anxious for nothing, but in everything by prayer and supplication, with thanksgiving, let your requests be made known to God" (Philippians 4:6). Consider the words of the psalmist. "Make a joyful shout to the LORD, all you lands! Serve the LORD with gladness; Come before His presence with singing. Know that the LORD, He is God; It is He who has made us, and not we ourselves; we are His people and the sheep of His pasture. Enter into His gates with thanksgiving, And into His courts with praise. Be thankful to Him, and bless His name. For the LORD is good; His mercy is everlasting, and His truth endures to all generations" (Psalm 100).

S – **Supplication-** Supplication comes from the word "supply." We often make requests of God, i.e., we ask God to supply us with various blessings. There are many things for which Christians ought to ask - wisdom, peace, patience, opportunities to teach, health, safety, enemies, etc. Brethren, don't forget to pray! Supplication includes what many refer to as a fifth type of prayer. That is a **prayer of intercession.** In this type of prayer, we ask God to intercede or care for another person of His creation.

Five Fingers of Prayer

Someone has come up with this interesting and memorable way of remembering for whom to pray. This is beautiful, and surely worth making the Five Finger Prayer a part of our lives. I regret that I do not know to whom to give credit.

1. Your thumb is nearest to you. So begin your prayers by praying for those closest to you. They are the easiest to remember. To pray for our loved ones is, as C. S. Lewis once said, a "sweet duty."

2. The next finger is the pointing finger. Pray for those who teach, instruct and heal. This includes teachers, doctors, elders and ministers. They need support and wisdom in pointing others in the right direction. Keep them in your prayers.

3. The next finger is the tallest finger. It reminds us of our leaders. Pray for the president, leaders in business and industry, and administrators. These people shape our nation and guide public opinion. They need God's guidance.

4. The fourth finger is our ring finger. Surprising to many is the fact that this is our weakest finger, as any piano teacher will testify. It should remind us to pray for those who are weak, in trouble or in pain. They need our prayers day and night. We cannot pray too much for them.

5. Lastly comes our little finger, the smallest finger of all. This is where we should place ourselves in relation to God and others. As the Bible says, "The least shall be the greatest among you." Your pinkie should remind you to pray for yourself.

By the time you have prayed for the other four groups, your own needs will be put into proper perspective and you will be able to pray for yourself more effectively. Should you find it hard to get to sleep tonight, remember the homeless who have no beds in which to lie.

Conclusion

Prayer is the way we communicate with God. We have the power to evoke the blessing of God to help us with the many problems that come our way. Isn't it good to know that God has allowed us this method of communication? James said, "Confess your trespasses to one another, and pray for one another, that you may be healed. The effective, fervent prayer of a righteous man avails much" (James 5:16).

Do you know of someone you need to be praying for today? Remember that Jesus sought a quiet secluded place to pray. It seems that our lives are so filled with rushing about that we do not take time to pray. We live in a very noisy world which distracts our concentration. Yet we can find a "quiet place." We can pray as we drive. We can pray at our desk or work station. We can pray with our families. We can pray when we are alone. We simply need to pray! I'm reminded of the words of the old hymn that says, *"Sweet hour of prayer, sweet hour of prayer! That calls me from a world of care, and bids me, at my Father's throne, make all my wants and wishes known. In seasons of distress and grief my soul has often found relief, and oft escaped the tempter's snare, by thy return sweet hour of prayer."* Let us search more diligently for that sweet hour of prayer. Amen!

Answered Prayer?

"They built a raunchy nightspot right next door to Saint Lukewarm Baptist Church of God in Christ. The good folks of SLBCOGIC decided to start a prayer vigil. Amazingly, the nightclub's business dwindled so much they had to close the doors. This wasn't altogether good news, you see; the owners of the nightclub brought a lawsuit against the members of SLBCOGIC, accusing them of ruining their business with their prayers. The attorneys for the church argued there was no way their prayers could have had any effect on the poor performance of the club. The judge agreed. He ruled in favor of Saint Lukewarm, saying, "while the nightclub owner strongly believes in the power of prayer, the church membership does not" (Dana Key, By Divine Design, Nashville, 1995, p. 13).

Just Go To God In Prayer
Frank Richey

When trials of life seem tough and unfair,
And days are filled with worry and care,
When problems persist and solace resists,
Just go to God in prayer.

When loved ones cause disappointment and pain,
And discouragement fills your days,
Pray that you might bear the darkest despair,
Just go to God in prayer.

When those that you love turn their backs on you,
And their lives leave you weary and stressed,
To Him you can cleave, for He'll never leave,
Just go to God in prayer.

When your sin is a burden that you bear each day
And guilt fills your heart at night,
Ask Him to forgive and your life for Him live,
Just go to God in prayer.

When sickness and grief take their toll on you,
And your soul is weary and worn,
When life seems unfair with the burdens you bear,
Just go to God in prayer.

When death of a loved one burdens your soul
And you feel all alone with grief,
In anguish you sigh, turn to God on high,
Just go to God in prayer.

Just go to God in prayer
Before the throne on high.
Every burden you bear, tell to God in prayer.
We know that He is nigh.

Prayer Quotes

"Don't pray for lighter burdens, but for stronger backs."

"To be a Christian without prayer is no more possible than to be alive without breathing."

"Pray as though everything depended on God. Work as though everything depended on you."

"Most people do not pray; they only beg."

"All prayers are answered if we are willing to admit that sometimes the answer is "no".

"A lot of kneeling will keep you in good standing."

Chapter 12

How We Worship—Lord's Supper

As we continue looking at "The Worship of the Church," we want to look at all the things we do in worship and show biblical authority for what we do. In this lesson, we want to consider "The Lord's Supper." The Lord's Supper should be of vital importance to a Christian. A perversion of our attitude in observing this supper can lead to spiritual death. Paul says, "Therefore whoever eats this bread or drinks this cup of the Lord in an unworthy manner will be guilty of the body and blood of the Lord" (1 Corinthians 11:27).

Origin and Authority of the Supper

As we embark on this study, we want to consider the authority we have to participate in this act of worship. Authority is defined as right, power, or jurisdiction. Let's look at what the Bible says.

The Lord's Supper was instituted by our Lord Jesus Christ. "And as they were eating, Jesus took bread, blessed and broke it, and gave it to the disciples and said, "Take, eat; this is My body." Then He took the cup, and gave thanks, and gave it to them, saying, "Drink from it, all of you. For this is My blood of the new covenant, which is shed for many for the remission of sins. But I say to you, I will not drink of this fruit of the vine from now on until that day when I drink it new with you in My Father's kingdom" (Matthew

26:26-29). We see from this passage that Jesus authorized the keeping of this part of our worship.

The keeping of the Lord's Supper was taught by the apostles. In fact, Jesus said that the disciples were to teach the converts to "observe all things that I have commanded you" (Matthew 28:20). As we saw in the passage in Matthew 26, Jesus told the disciples to partake of this spiritual feast.

The apostle Paul spoke about the keeping of this Supper when he said, "For I received from the Lord that which I also delivered to you: that the Lord Jesus on the same night in which He was betrayed took bread; and when He had given thanks, He broke it and said, "Take, eat; this is My body which is broken for you; do this in remembrance of Me." In the same manner He also took the cup after supper, saying, "This cup is the new covenant in My blood. This do, as often as you drink it, in remembrance of Me." For as often as you eat this bread and drink this cup, you proclaim the Lord's death till He comes." (1 Corinthians 11:23-26).

It was practiced by the New Testament church. In Troas, Paul came together with the saints to partake of the Lord's Supper. "Now on the first day of the week, when the disciples came together to break bread, Paul, ready to depart the next day, spoke to them and continued his message until midnight" (Acts 20:7).

It was received from the Lord. Paul said, "For I received from the Lord that which I also delivered to you: that the Lord Jesus on the same night in which He was betrayed took bread" (1 Corinthians 11:23).

The Design of the Lord's Supper

What do we mean by design of the Lord's Supper? We mean that Christ designed the Supper for specific purposes. Let's look at those purposes.

The Lord's Supper was designed as a remembrance, a memorial to Jesus Christ. "…and when He had given thanks, He broke it and said, "Take, eat; this is My body which is broken for you; **do this in remembrance of Me.**" In the same manner He also took the cup after supper, saying, "This cup is the new covenant in My blood. This do, as often as you drink it, in remembrance of Me" (1 Corinthians 11:24-25).

The Lord's Supper is a time of anticipation. We should look forward to each Sunday when we can have this supper with Christ. But I say to you, I will not drink of this fruit of the vine from now on until that day when I drink it new with you in My Father's kingdom" (Matthew 26:29). In this passage, we see that in a figurative sense, Christ is with us as we engage in this Supper together. H. Leo Boles says, "in My Father's kingdom– (refers to) the church which was established on the day of Pentecost … The term 'drink' is used figuratively to express that communion which Jesus has with his disciples while they are eating the Lord's Supper."

The Lord's Supper is a fellowship or communion. Paul said, "The cup of blessing which we bless, is it not the communion of the blood of Christ? The bread which we break, is it not the communion of the body of Christ" (1 Corinthians 10:16)? Communion is defined as: Fellowship; joint participation; intimacy. (Strong's Greek Words of the New Testament). When we partake of the Communion (the Lord's Supper), we are engaged in a joint participation of this spiritual feast with Jesus Christ. It is a time of fellowship with Christ. Fellowship simply means, "Something we do together." Jesus said that "…where two or three are gathered together in My name, I am there in the midst of them" (Matthew 18:20). I often wonder if we believe this.

When we partake of the Lord's Supper we make a proclamation. "For as often as you eat this bread and drink this cup, you proclaim the Lord's death till He comes" (1 Corinthians 11:26). A proclamation is an announcement, publication, declaration. The gospel must be proclaimed to the world. Paul said to the Athenians, "for as I was passing through and considering the objects of your worship, I even found an altar with this inscription: TO THE UNKNOWN GOD. Therefore, the One whom you worship without knowing, Him **I proclaim** to you" (Acts 17:23). The Lord's Supper is a proclamation to the world of God's love, grace and salvation. It is a proclamation of our faith, courage and zeal as we partake of the emblems of the Supper.

The Lord's Supper is the dedication of the new covenant. Jesus said the "cup" was the new covenant in His blood. "In the same manner He also took the cup after supper, saying, "This cup is the new covenant in My blood. This do, as often as you drink it, in remembrance of Me" (1 Corinthians 11:25). A covenant suggests sealing or ratifying an agreement. The Lord's Supper is a covenant we have with God. This covenant is sealed with the blood of Christ.

Jesus Christ is the mediator of a "better covenant." "But now He has obtained a more excellent ministry, inasmuch as He is also Mediator of a better covenant, which was established on better promises. For if that first covenant had been faultless, then no place would have been sought for a second. Because finding fault with them, He says: "Behold, the days are coming, says the LORD, when I will make a new covenant with the house of Israel and with the house of Judah" (Hebrews 8:6-8).

That covenant was sealed with the blood of Christ. The Bible teaches that for a will to be confirmed, there must be the death of the one who made the will. We see this in Hebrews 9:16-17, where the Hebrew writer says, "For where there is a testament, there must also of necessity be the death of the testator. For a testament is in force after men are dead, since it has no power at all while the testator lives." Christ died on the cross so that the New Covenant, the Last Will and Testament of Jesus Christ, could come into existence.

The Lord's Supper is obedience to Christ. "And as they were eating, Jesus took bread, blessed and broke it, and gave it to the disciples and said, "Take, eat; this is My body." Then He took the cup, and gave thanks, and gave it to them, saying, "Drink from it, all of you" (Matthew 26:26-28). This was not a mere suggestion on the part of Christ, but a command to be carried out by all Christians of all ages. Given in the very shadow of the cross, Christ said "Take, eat" and "Drink from it, all of you."

The Manner of Observance

We must examine ourselves. "But let a man examine himself, and so let him eat of the bread and drink of the cup" (1 Corinthians 11:28). Self-examination is a vital part of partaking of the Lord's Supper. The manner in which we partake is of great importance to Christ. Notice the next point.

We must observe it worthily. This describes the manner in which we partake of it. The apostle Paul wrote much about the Lord's Supper in his first letter to the Corinthians. Notice this passage: "Therefore whoever eats this bread or drinks this cup of the Lord in an unworthy manner will be guilty of the body and blood of the Lord. But let a man examine himself, and so let him eat of the bread and drink of the cup. For he who eats and drinks in an unworthy manner eats and drinks judgment to himself, not discerning the Lord's body" (1 Corinthians 11:27-29).

To partake of the Supper in a light-hearted, flippant manner suggests that one does not know the significance of the Supper or does not care about the significance of the Supper. It further suggests that one does not discern the Lord's body as he/she partakes. I have observed people when the Lord's Supper is being passed around. Some are chewing gum, giggling, talking, playing with the babies, etc. It is sometimes so very obvious that they are not fully aware of the significance of the Supper, nor of their actions and the manner in which they partake of the Supper. The seriousness of this is seen in 1 Corinthians 11:30, where Paul says, "For this reason many are weak and sick among you, and many sleep." As a result of partaking of the Lord's Supper in an irreverent manner, Paul said "many are weak" (spiritually) "and sick" (spiritually), "and many sleep" (they are dead spiritually).

We must observe it regularly. The New Testament church had the Supper on the first day of the week. "Now on the first day of the week, when the disciples came together to break bread, Paul, ready to depart the next day, spoke to them and continued his message until midnight" (Acts 20:7).

Question: How often do we have a first day of the week? The first day of the week was the common meeting day of the early church. This is seen in 1 Corinthians 16:2, where the saints were told that on the "first day of the week let each one of you lay something aside, storing up as he may prosper, that there be no collections when I come." The Christians in the New Testament met on the first day of the week and they were not to forsake this assembly. "...not forsaking the assembling of ourselves together, as is the manner of some, but exhorting one another, and so much the more as you see the Day approaching. For if we sin willfully after we have received the knowledge of the truth, there no longer remains a sacrifice for sins" (Hebrews 10:25-26). If the New Testament Christians came together on the first day of the week to partake of the Lord's Supper, in order to be in compliance with the will of Christ, we also must come together on the first day of the week to partake of the Lord's Supper.

Scholars Agree That The New Testament Church Partook Of The Lord's Supper Every Week.

Justin Martyr (ca. 150 AD) records how Christians assembled on Sunday and partook of the Supper (Apology I, p. 67).

"...the early church writers from Barnabas, Justin Martyr, Irenaeus, to Clement of Alexandria, Origen and Cyprian, all with one consent, declare that the church observed the first day of the week. They are equally agreed that the Lord's Supper was observed weekly, on the first day of the week" (B. W. Johnson, People's New Testament).

"The observance of the Lord's Supper seems to have been administered every Lord's day; and probably no professed Christian absented themselves..." Thomas Scott, Presbyterian (Commentary on Acts 20:7).

"This also is an important example of weekly communion as the practice of the first Christians" A. C. Hervey, Episcopalian, (Commentary on Acts 20:7).

"It is well known that the primitive Christians administered the Eucharist (the Lord's Supper) every Lord's day" P. Doddridge, Congregationalist, (Notes on Acts 20:7).

We Must Be Careful Not to Pervert the Lord's Supper

The church at Corinth was guilty of this. The apostle Paul said, "Therefore when you come together in one place, it is not to eat the Lord's Supper. For in eating, each one takes his own supper ahead of others; and one is hungry and another is drunk. What! Do you not have houses to eat and drink in? Or do you despise the church of

God and shame those who have nothing? What shall I say to you? Shall I praise you in this? I do not praise you" (1 Corinthians 11:20-22). We must never be guilty of making a mockery of the Lord's Supper by turning it into a common meal!

Our allegiance must be to Christ in order to partake of the Lord's Supper. Again, Paul says, "You cannot drink the cup of the Lord and the cup of demons; you cannot partake of the Lord's Table and of the table of demons. Or do we provoke the Lord to jealousy? Are we stronger than He" (1 Corinthians 10:21-22)? Again, this is a part of the self-examination mentioned earlier. We must belong to Christ, be in His Kingdom, and give our full allegiance to Christ before we participate in this Supper.

Many churches today are perverting the Lord's Supper and making it a common meal instead of a spiritual meal. Some conservative, non-institutional churches of Christ are doing this. From what I understand, the Lord's Supper is not a time to mix and mingle, eat as much bread and drink as much "fruit of the vine" as you wish. This does not sound like a spiritual feast, focused on the sacrifice of Jesus for our sins!

Three Views of the Lord's Supper

The Lord's Supper is a time to <u>LOOK BACKWARD</u>. "In the same manner He also took the cup after supper, saying, "This cup is the new covenant in My blood. This do, as often as you drink it, in remembrance of Me" (1 Corinthians 11:25). When we take the Lord's Supper, it is a time of reflection on the death of Christ—we remember Him! He left heaven, came to the earth, lived among men, and was crucified for the sins of mankind. We need to focus our minds on that sacrifice for our sins and truly appreciate the sacrifice made for us so we can have the hope of a heavenly home. We need to try to picture Christ on the cross, see Him as he endured the pain of the crucifixion—for you! I believe this is what Christ had in mind as He said, "do this in remembrance of Me."

The Lord's Supper is a time to LOOK FORWARD. "For as often as you eat this bread and drink this cup, you proclaim the Lord's death **till He comes**" (1 Corinthians 11:26). Jesus said he would drink of the fruit of the vine with us in the kingdom (Matthew 26:29). We should look forward every week to the time that we can commune with Christ, knowing that He is with us as we partake of the communion. This should also point us to the time when we will commune with Christ in heaven throughout all eternity.

The Lord's Supper is a time to LOOK INWARD. As we have already mentioned, we are to examine ourselves when eating the Lord's Supper. "But let a man examine himself, and so let him eat of the bread and drink of the cup. For he who eats and drinks in an unworthy manner eats and drinks judgment to himself, not discerning the Lord's body" (1 Corinthians 11:28-29). Self-examination involves looking inward to see what kind of man or woman we are and whether we are what Christ wants us to be. If by self-examination we realize that we are not in accordance to the will of Christ, then we need to make changes spiritually so that our lives coincide with the will of Christ before we partake of the Lord's Supper.

Seven Things to Remember During the Lord's Supper

This little mnemonic device will help one to focus on the sacrifice of Christ as He died on the cross. It will help one to "do this in remembrance of Me."

1—**One Lord**
2—**Two thieves**
3—**Three crosses**
4—**Four soldiers dividing the garments of Christ**
5—**Five wounds of Christ** **(1)** Crown on His head, **(2)** His beaten back, **(3)** Nails in His hands, **(4)** Nails in His feet, **(5)** Wound from the spear thrust into His side
6—**Darkness from the 6th to the 9th hour.**
7—**Seven sayings of Christ on the cross.** **(1)** *"Father forgive them, for they know not what they do."* **(2)** *"Today you will be with me in paradise."* **(3)** *"Behold your son: behold your mother."* **(4)** *"Eloi Eloi lama sabachthani"* [My God, My God, why have You forsaken Me?] **(5)** *"I thirst."* **(6)** *"It is finished."* **(7)** *"Into your hands I commit My Spirit."*

Conclusion

There is no place on earth that one can feel closer to Christ than when one partakes of the Lord's Supper with other Christians in the manner prescribed by our Lord. We can be assured that Christ is there with us, and we are reminded that someday we will be able to commune with Christ throughout all eternity.

Chapter 13

How We Worship—Preaching

"For since, in the wisdom of God, the world through wisdom did not know God, it pleased God through the foolishness of the message preached to save those who believe. For Jews request a sign, and Greeks seek after wisdom; but we preach Christ crucified, to the Jews a stumbling block and to the Greeks foolishness, but to those who are called, both Jews and Greeks, Christ the power of God and the wisdom of God. Because the foolishness of God is wiser than men, and the weakness of God is stronger than men" (1 Corinthians 1:21-25).

From the preceding passage, we see that the purpose of preaching is the salvation of men's souls. Preaching is certainly a biblical subject. We find the words "preach," "preacher" and "preaching" a total of 147 times in the Bible along with various similar expressions such as "spoke" and "speech" to show many more times the importance of this biblical topic.

Webster defines the word "preach" as: To expound upon in writing or speech; especially, to urge acceptance of or compliance with (specified religious or moral principles). To deliver a sermon or advice. The Greek word for preach is khrussw (kerusso), {kay-roos'-so} It means: To herald (as a public crier), especially divine truth (the gospel), preach, proclaim, publish.

Preaching may be a lost art in many churches, but is still God's chosen method of delivering His gospel to those for whom He died. The truth must be boldly proclaimed. Yet, the proclamation must be made clear for all to hear and apply.

While many think that preaching is a relic of old churches, the New Testament church thrives on the preaching of the gospel of Jesus Christ. When the truths of God are presented, we should humbly submit to God's will in the spoken word of God's messengers.

Preaching is the presentation of scriptural truth. It is not to be the opinion of the preacher, a commentary on current events, or the riding of some hobby that the preacher has. Sound preaching is the presentation of the holy word of God in a spoken form for the purpose of bringing about change in the hearers. Its nature is to sway, convince, argue, expound, reprove, rebuke, exhort and reason from the word of God in order to change men for the better. The alien sinner needs to be changed into a baptized believer. The believer needs to be changed into an active worker, and the strong Christian is in need of growing even more in order to please God. If you ever think you know all that you need to know, you become stagnant and worldly pollutions will creep into your life.

Preaching is God's plan for the proclamation of His word to mankind. It's that simple. It is God's plan. Man cannot improve upon it. Preaching is the transmitting of God's word to a lost and dying world. Preaching serves to edify the believer, giving him or her strength to meet the demands of a hectic daily life. It brings about growth for the building up of His church on this earth. Preaching the truth is necessary for the survival of the Lord's church!

Preaching is a storming of the will...an assault on the mind of the individual to bring about change for good and conformity to the gospel of Christ. Preaching differs from teaching in that while teaching is instructive and explanatory; preaching proclaims a truth with the emphasis and desire of acceptance for that truth.

Authority For Preaching In The Assembly

From a study of the scriptures on preaching, there does not seem to be a wrong place to preach. Jesus told his disciples to "...Go into all the world and preach the gospel to every creature" (Mark 16:15). Those that were scattered as a result of the persecution in Judea, "went everywhere preaching the word" (Acts 8:4).

The apostle Paul told the church in Rome that "...I am ready to preach the gospel to you..." (Romans 1:15). What better place to preach to Christians than in the assembly of the church. But perhaps the best passage to show that preaching was a part of the worship of the New Testament church is found in Acts 20:7, a verse we often use to point out the importance of partaking of the Lord's Supper in worship. In this passage, we find that Paul spoke in the assembly of the church. We are told "...Paul, ready to depart the next day, spoke to them and continued his message until midnight" (Acts 20:7).

Purpose of Preaching

We preach to save those who believe. Paul tells us this when he says, "For since, in the wisdom of God, the world through wisdom did not know God, it pleased God through the foolishness of **the message preached to save those who believe**" (1 Corinthians 1:21).

We preach to bring about change. Preaching by its very nature is designed to bring about change in the hearer. Paul said to Timothy, "Preach the word! Be ready in season and out of season. Reprove, rebuke, exhort, with all longsuffering and teaching" (2 Timothy 4:2). Reprove means to convince, tell a fault. Rebuke means to censure, admonish, forbid. Exhort means to invite, invoke, beseech, and call for. All of these things involve change!

We preach to turn back those who have turned from the truth. Paul again told Timothy that many people would "...not endure sound doctrine, but according to their own desires, because they have itching ears, they will heap up for themselves teachers; and they will turn their ears away from the truth, and be turned aside to fables" (2 Timothy 4:3-4).

We preach to save men's souls. When we preach God's word, we believe what James said concerning the word of God: "Therefore lay aside all filthiness and overflow of wickedness, and receive with meekness the implanted word, which is able to save your souls" (James 1:21).

We preach to enlighten the hearers. All have sinned (Romans 3:23) and therefore need to understand God's will for man. We are told to "confess our sins" (1 John 1:9). We are to know what God expects of man. We are not to be "conformed to this world, but transformed by the renewing of your mind..." (Romans 12:2).

We preach to turn men from darkness to light. Paul said that they preached "...preach to you that you should turn from these useless things to the living God..." (Acts 14:15).

We preach to urge men to repent. "Then Peter said to them, "Repent, and let every one of you be baptized in the name of Jesus Christ for the remission of sins; and you shall receive the gift of the Holy Spirit" (Acts 2:38).

We preach to tell men that God can and will forgive them. Christ loved us and died for us even when we were in sin and in opposition to God. "But God demonstrates His own love toward us, in that while we were still sinners, Christ died for us" (Romans 5:8). We are also told, "In Him we have redemption through His blood, the forgiveness of sins, according to the riches of His grace" (Ephesians

1:7). Also in Acts 13:38, we are told, "Therefore let it be known to you, brethren, that through this Man is preached to you the forgiveness of sins."

We preach to tell men the consequences of rejecting the word of God. "For we must all appear before the judgment seat of Christ, that each one may receive the things done in the body, according to what he has done, whether good or bad" (2 Corinthians 5:10).

We preach to become stronger spiritually. It is by God's word that we grow, and preaching is a sharing of God's word. Peter said, "Therefore, laying aside all malice, all deceit, hypocrisy, envy, and all evil speaking, as newborn babes, desire the pure milk of the word, that you may grow thereby" (1 Peter 2:1-2). The Hebrew writer pointed out that some needed to be teachers but had not developed spiritually to the point of teaching. "For though by this time you ought to be teachers, you need someone to teach you again the first principles of the oracles of God; and you have come to need milk and not solid food" (Hebrews 5:12).

We preach that man might have faith in the power of God. "And I, brethren, when I came to you, did not come with excellence of speech or of wisdom declaring to you the testimony of God. For I determined not to know anything among you except Jesus Christ and Him crucified. I was with you in weakness, in fear, and in much trembling. And my speech and my preaching were not with persuasive words of human wisdom, but in demonstration of the Spirit and of power, that your faith should not be in the wisdom of men but in the power of God" (1 Corinthians 2:1-5).

What Is To Be Preached?

God's word is to be preached. Paul told Timothy to "Preach the word! Be ready in season and out of season. Convince, rebuke, exhort, with all longsuffering and teaching" (2 Timothy 4:2). If preachers today would spend more of their preaching time in the scriptures rather than in the Joke Book or Book of 10,000 Sermon Illustrations, Chicken Soup books or leave off the multitude of cute stories that tickle the senses, and just preach God's word, we would be better off. Obviously, illustrations can drive home a point, but we need to be sure the point is what is presented in God's word, and not the illustration itself.

Peter's sermon is an example of what was preached. One of the often overlooked passages in the Bible is the 4th chapter of Acts, where Peter gives a defense for the healing of the lame man mentioned in chapter three. In this defense, Peter gives a great sermon outline—an example inspired of God. Notice the passage and the outline of the sermon.

Acts 4:8-12- "Then Peter, filled with the Holy Spirit, said to them, "Rulers of the people and elders of Israel: If we this day are judged for a good deed done to a helpless man, by what means he has been made well, let it be known to you all, and to all the people of Israel, that by the…

1. "Name of Jesus Christ of Nazareth,"- **Authority of Christ.**
2. "Whom you crucified," – **The death of Christ and the purpose of His death.**
3. "Whom God raised from the dead," - **The resurrection of Christ from the dead.**
4. "By Him this man stands here before you whole" – **The power of God.**
5. "This is the stone which was rejected by you builders, which has become the chief cornerstone." – **Christ is the cornerstone of our spiritual house.**
6. "Nor is there salvation in any other, for there is no other name under heaven given among men by which we must be saved." – **Salvation is in no other name!**

This gospel sermon "will preach" just as it did 2,000 years ago. The message of the ancient gospel is always contemporary.

We are to preach the Gospel. Ninety-seven times we find "gospel" and "preached" in the same verse. One cannot preach the gospel without preaching God's word, and one cannot preach God's word without preaching the gospel (the Good News) of Jesus Christ. Paul said, "...I have fully preached the gospel of Christ" (Romans 15:19). He also tells us that the gospel during the first century "...was preached to every creature under heaven..." (Colossians 1:23).

The Need To Hear Preaching

Preaching will not accomplish its purpose unless there are people to hear those things preached. We mentioned at the beginning of this study that preaching by its very nature is to produce change—change in what we do, where we go, what we say, how we worship, and to deepen our relationship with God. This can only happen when we hear God's word and that word motivates us to change—to do what God says. Jesus said, "Not everyone who says to Me, 'Lord, Lord,' shall enter the kingdom of heaven, but he who does the will of My Father in heaven" (Matthew 7:21). James said, "But be doers of the word, and not hearers only, deceiving yourselves" (James 1:22).

We need to hear the gospel preached because all have sinned. "for all have sinned and fall short of the glory of God" (Romans 3:23).

We need to hear the gospel because we all need to be transformed spiritually. Paul told the Romans in chapter twelve at verses one and two, that we need to be transformed rather than conformed to the world, and we do this when we present our bodies as a living sacrifice, holy and acceptable to God. As I've said many times, this is a "brain thing," a mental determination to be pleasing to God and to serve Him faithfully.

We need to hear the consequences of refusing God's word. There are eternal consequences at stake—the very existence of one's eternal soul! When this is fully comprehended, one should have a desire to spend eternity in heaven, rather than hell. Paul said, "For we must all appear before the judgment seat of Christ, that each one may receive the things done in the body, according to what he has done, whether good or bad" (2 Corinthians 5:10).

The Need For Preaching Destroys The Argument For The Direct Operation Of The Holy Spirit

If the Holy Spirit operates on us directly and apart from the word of God, then there is no need for preaching. However, this is not the case and this is not taught in the Bible. God does not save man through the direct operation of the Holy Spirit, but through His word.

We must hear of the Father before we can come to Him. Jesus said, "It is written in the prophets, 'And they shall all be taught by God.' Therefore everyone who has heard and learned from the Father comes to Me" (John 6:45). We must hear and learn before we can come to the Father. We are not saved by the Holy Spirit making a personal appearance and directly convicting us of sin and providing salvation. We are saved through the word of God.

The Holy Spirit did direct the apostles into the complete truth that they were to use to bring men to God. Yes, the Holy Spirit saves us, but not through a direct operation. It was the work of the Holy Spirit to guide and direct the apostles, as inspired men, as they recorded the word of God. Jesus, speaking of the imminent coming of the Holy Spirit, said, "And when He has come, He will convict the world of sin, and of righteousness, and of judgment: of sin, because they do not believe in Me; of righteousness, because I go to My Father and you see Me no more; of judgment, because the ruler of this world is judged. "I still have many things to say to you, but you cannot bear them now. However, when He, the Spirit of truth, has come**, He will guide you into all truth**; for He will not speak on His own authority, but whatever He hears He will speak; and He will tell you things to come" (John 16:8-13).

We believe through the word. Jesus while in the garden shortly before His crucifixion, prayed to the Father and said, "I do not pray for these alone, but also for those who will believe in Me through their word" (John 17:20). Whose word? The word that was preached by the apostles as they shared the gospel with the world.

God's word will save us from our sins. It is through God's word that we know and understand our spiritual condition and are able to realize the need to conform to the word of God. It is the word of God that will free us from the bondage of sin. "Then Jesus said to those Jews who believed Him, "If you abide in My word, you are My disciples indeed. And you shall know the truth, and the truth shall make you free" (John 8:31-32).

Conclusion

Let us never underestimate the power of God's spoken word. God chose this method of instruction above all others for the purpose of sharing His word with a lost and dying world.

Preaching and preachers are made fun of through the media. They are laughed at and mocked. The message and the messenger are depicted as ridiculous, antiquated, and stupid. Much of this caricature has been brought on by preachers with their display of showmanship, supposed miracles, and powers of a salesman, not unlike the used car salesman on television.

But let us never forget that God chose preaching to save mankind from eternal destruction. Again, Paul said, "For since, in the wisdom of God, the world through wisdom did not know God, it pleased God through the foolishness of the message preached to save those who believe" (1 Corinthians 1:21). Also remember that that which seems foolish to man is a part of the plan of God in all His wisdom.

Chapter 14

How We Worship—The Contribution

"Will a man rob God? Yet you have robbed Me! But you say, 'In what way have we robbed You?' In tithes and offerings" (Malachi 3:8).

In this chapter, we want to consider the subject of the collection as a part of our worship to God. The modern concept of "money grubbing preachers" trying to squeeze money out of needy widows is the idea that many have of this part of our worship. This is far from the picture painted in the Bible of the concept of giving.

Under the Old Law, the Jews gave a minimum of 10% of their income, along with first fruits and portions of their vineyards, grain fields, and olives to those in need. Some have estimated that the Jews gave one-third of their income to the Lord.

This begs the question…When the Jews were converted to Christianity, do you think they did less for the Lord under the law of Christ than they did under the Mosaical Law?

Many today want a religion that costs them nothing. Consider the attitude of David in this matter.

2 Samuel 24:18-24 "And Gad came that day to David and said to him, 'Go up, erect an altar to the LORD on the threshing floor of Araunah the Jebusite.' So David, according to the word of Gad, went up as the LORD commanded. Now Araunah looked, and saw the king and his servants coming toward him. So Araunah went out and bowed before the king with his face to the ground. Then Araunah said, 'Why has my lord the king come to his servant?' And David said, 'To buy the threshing floor from you, to build an altar to the LORD, that the plague may be withdrawn from the people.' Now Araunah said to David, 'Let my lord the king take and offer up whatever seems good to him. Look, here are oxen for burnt sacrifice, and threshing implements and the yokes of the oxen for wood. All these, O king, Araunah has given to the king.' And Araunah said to the king, 'May the LORD your God accept you.' Then the king said to Araunah, 'No, but I will surely buy it from you for a price; nor will I offer burnt offerings to the LORD my God with that which costs me nothing.' So David bought the threshing floor and the oxen for fifty shekels of silver."

The New Testament Church Contributed To The Work Of The Church

The New Testament Church had all things in common. Acts 2:42-45 "And they continued steadfastly in the apostles' doctrine and fellowship, in the breaking of bread, and in prayers. Then fear came upon every soul, and many wonders and signs were done through the apostles. Now all who believed were together, and had all things in common, and sold their possessions and goods, and divided them among all, as anyone had need."

The New Testament church laid money at the apostle's feet. Acts 4:34-35 "Nor was there anyone among them who lacked; for all who were possessors of lands or houses sold them, and brought the proceeds of the things that were sold, and laid them at the apostles' feet; and they distributed to each as anyone had need."

When contributed, the money became God's money to be used as God would have it to be used. Acts 5:1-4 "But a certain man named Ananias, with Sapphira his wife, sold a possession. And he kept back part of the proceeds, his wife also being aware of it, and brought a certain part and laid it at the apostles' feet. But Peter said, 'Ananias, why has Satan filled your heart to lie to the Holy Spirit and keep back part of the price of the land for yourself? While it remained, was it not your own? And after it was sold, was it not in your own control? Why have you conceived this thing in your heart? You have not lied to men but to God.'"

The contribution was necessary to care for needy members. Acts 6:1-4 "Now in those days, when the number of the disciples was multiplying, there arose a complaint against the Hebrews by the Hellenists, because their widows were neglected in the daily distribution. Then the twelve summoned the multitude of the disciples and said, 'It is not desirable that we should leave the word of God and serve tables. Therefore, brethren, seek out from among you seven men of good reputation, full of the Holy Spirit and wisdom, whom we may appoint over this business; but we will give ourselves continually to prayer and to the ministry of the word.'"

1 Corinthians 16:1-2 "Now concerning the collection for the saints, as I have given orders to the churches of Galatia, so you must do also: On the first day of the week let each one of you lay something aside, storing up as he may prosper, that there be no collections when I come."

Contribution Was Necessary To Support The Preaching Of The Gospel

A contribution was necessary to supply the needs of the church at Antioch to send men out on the first missionary journey. Acts 13:1-4 " Now in the church that was at Antioch there were certain prophets and teachers: Barnabas, Simeon who was called Niger, Lucius of Cyrene, Manaen who had been brought up with Herod the tetrarch, and Saul. As they ministered to the Lord and fasted, the Holy Spirit said, "Now separate to Me Barnabas and Saul for the work to which I have called them." Then, having fasted and prayed, and laid hands on them, they sent them away. So, being sent out by the Holy Spirit, they went down to Seleucia, and from there they sailed to Cyprus."

The collection was used to support a preacher. 1 Corinthians 9:1-7 "Am I not an apostle? Am I not free? Have I not seen Jesus Christ our Lord? Are you not my work in the Lord? If I am not an apostle to others, yet doubtless I am to you. For you are the seal of my apostleship in the Lord. My defense to those who examine me is this: Do we have no right to eat and drink? Do we have no right to take along a believing wife, as do also the other apostles, the brothers of the Lord, and Cephas? Or is it only Barnabas and I who have no right to refrain from working? Who ever goes to war at his own expense? Who plants a vineyard and does not eat of its fruit? Or who tends a flock and does not drink of the milk of the flock?"

The contribution could be used to support an elder. 1 Timothy 5:17-18 "Let the elders who rule well be counted worthy of double honor, especially those who labor in the word and doctrine. For the Scripture says, 'You shall not muzzle an ox while it treads out the grain,' and, "The laborer is worthy of his wages.'"

From the above scriptures, it seems evident that the church has the right to take up a collection and to support the work of the church.

Objections To The Contribution

Some argue that collections were to be taken up at home. If a collection was taken up at home, it still had to be "collected" by the church at some point to do the work of the church.

Some argue that we must know a specific need before we take up a collection. The church at Corinth had a treasury, but did not support Paul. Did they know his need? Did they refuse to support him? Paul did not ask them for support and they did not give him support. If they had a treasury and Paul needed support, according to the thinking of some, they would have had to take up a collection specifically for Paul's support.

2 Corinthians 11:8-9 "I robbed other churches, taking wages from them to minister to you. And when I was present with you, and in need, I was a burden to no one, for what I lacked the brethren who came from Macedonia supplied. And in everything I kept myself from being burdensome to you, and so I will keep myself."

2 Corinthians 12:13 "For what is it in which you were inferior to other churches, except that I myself was not burdensome to you? Forgive me this wrong!"

1 Corinthians 9:11-12 "If we have sown spiritual things for you, is it a great thing if we reap your material things? If others are partakers of this right over you, are we not even more? Nevertheless we have not used this right, but endure all things lest we hinder the gospel of Christ."

The Church Has Permanent Responsibilities Which Necessitate A Permanent Treasury

Permanent responsibilities demand permanent treasuries. Among those permanent responsibilities are:

The benevolent needs may be permanent. 1 Timothy 5:9-10 "Do not let a widow under sixty years old be taken into the number, and not unless she has been the wife of one man, well reported for good works: if she has brought up children, if she has lodged strangers, if she has washed the saints' feet, if she has relieved the afflicted, if she has diligently followed every good work."

Support for preaching the gospel is a permanent matter, not a temporary arrangement. 1 Corinthians 9:11-12 "If we have sown spiritual things for you, is it a great thing if we reap your material things? If others are partakers of this right over you, are we not even more? Nevertheless we have not used this right, but endure all things lest we hinder the gospel of Christ."

There is always a need to do the Lord's work. It is impractical to have to take up a collection every time a need arises, especially in view of the scriptural authority for a treasury.

Four Principles Of Giving

1. Giving is a matter of the heart. "But this I say: He who sows sparingly will also reap sparingly, and he who sows bountifully will also reap bountifully" (2 Corinthians 9:6). The attitude of our heart toward God may well determine how we give and how much we give to the Lord. Other passages that teach this principle are:

2 Corinthians 8:7 "But as you abound in everything—in faith, in speech, in knowledge, in all diligence, and in your love for us—see that you abound in this grace also."

2 Corinthians 8:19 "and not only that, but who was also chosen by the churches to travel with us with this gift, which is administered by us to the glory of the Lord Himself and to show your ready mind,"

2. Giving is a matter of the will. The Corinthians desired (willed) to give to the needy saints in Jerusalem. "And in this I give advice:

It is to your advantage not only to be doing what you began and were desiring to do a year ago" (2 Corinthians 8:10).

The Corinthians were willing to share liberally. Paul said, "While, through the proof of this ministry, they glorify God for the obedience of your confession to the gospel of Christ, and for your liberal sharing with them and all men" (2 Corinthians 9:13).

The story of the rich young ruler demonstrates that he was not willing to give. 'Now a certain ruler asked Him, saying, "Good Teacher, what shall I do to inherit eternal life?' So Jesus said to him, 'Why do you call Me good? No one is good but One, that is, God. You know the commandments: 'Do not commit adultery,' 'Do not murder,' 'Do not steal,' 'Do not bear false witness,' 'Honor your father and your mother.' And he said, 'All these things I have kept from my youth.' So when Jesus heard these things, He said to him, 'You still lack one thing. Sell all that you have and distribute to the poor, and you will have treasure in heaven; and come, follow Me.' But when he heard this, he became very sorrowful, for he was very rich. And when Jesus saw that he became very sorrowful, He said, 'How hard it is for those who have riches to enter the kingdom of God! For it is easier for a camel to go through the eye of a needle than for a rich man to enter the kingdom of God.' And those who heard it said, 'Who then can be saved?' But He said, 'The things which are impossible with men are possible with God'" (Luke 18:18-27).

3. Giving is a matter of faith. We give in order that we might reap bountifully. **2 Corinthians 9:6** "But this I say: He who sows sparingly will also reap sparingly, and he who sows bountifully will also reap bountifully."

We also give so that we might abound in grace. **2 Corinthians 8:7** "But as you abound in everything—in faith, in speech, in knowledge, in all diligence, and in your love for us—see that you abound in this grace also."

We give to the glory of the Lord. **2 Corinthians 8:19** "and not only that, but who was also chosen by the churches to travel with us with this gift, which is administered by us to the glory of the Lord Himself and to show your ready mind,"

4. Giving Is A Matter Of Emotion. We are to have the emotion of cheer and joy when we give to the Lord and not begrudge what we give. God loves a cheerful giver. Notice 2 Corinthians 9:7. "So let each one give as he purposes in his heart, not grudgingly or of necessity; for God loves a cheerful giver."

Our giving should also be **a matter of joy**. Even when we are in poverty, we can rejoice if we can help others. Speaking of the churches of Macedonia, Paul told the Corinthians, "that in a great trial of affliction the abundance of their joy and their deep poverty abounded in the riches of their liberality" (2 Corinthians 8:2).

When we give properly, **we prove our love to our Lord.** Paul said, "Therefore show to them, and before the churches the proof of your love and of our boasting on your behalf" (2 Corinthians 8:24).

Conclusion

May we ever give to God as He would have us to give and never fail in supporting the work of the Lord and His church! The contribution is not a matter of God needing our money, but our need to sacrifice to God in order that His will might be accomplished on earth.

Epilogue

The Bible teaches that Jesus Christ came to the earth to save men (Luke 19:10). A part of this plan for the salvation of man was that Christ would build His church (Matthew 16:13-18). The desire of every church and every individual should be to practice New Testament Christianity. In order to do this, we must worship God as the Christians of the first century worshiped. We believe that the only way man can know how to worship God is to go back to the Bible and simply do what the Bible says. In order to do this, we must give up all preconceived ideas about religion that might inhibit our returning to the Church of the New Testament.

The Lord's Church was established on the first Pentecost after the resurrection of Jesus. This is recorded for us in the second chapter of the Book of Acts. Peter seems to be the principal speaker on this occasion and in his sermon, convicted the hearers of Christ's death. Realizing their unsaved condition, and desiring to be saved from their sins, the people "said to Peter and the rest of the apostles, Men and brethren, what shall we do" (Acts 2:37). Peter's response to them was, "Repent, and let every one of you be baptized in the name of Jesus Christ for the remission of sins; and you shall receive the gift of the Holy Ghost" (Acts 2:38). Those who desired to be members of Christ's church and have their sins remitted were baptized for remission of sins. These first converts were the first members of the Lord's church. "And the Lord added to the church daily those who were being saved" (Acts 2:47).

The Bible teaches that Christ planned the church before the world came into existence. "He chose us in Him before the foundation of the world," and the manifold wisdom of God was "made known by the church" (Ephesians 1:4; 3:10). The church was so important to Christ that He died for it. Speaking of the church in the Book of Acts, Paul said, "He purchased (it) with His own blood". Paul also says the church is "the pillar and ground of the truth" (Acts 20:28; 1 Timothy 3:15).

The denominational concept of Christ's church is totally different from the picture we find in the New Testament. Denominationalism teaches that we can all believe different things and be saved. However, the Bible teaches that there is "one faith" (Ephesians 4:5), and "one church" (Ephesians 4:4; Ephesians 1: 22-23). Who is right, God or man? Jesus died for His church (Acts 20:28), not a church that bears the name of some man! Denominationalism teaches that many churches have come into existence in the past three hundred years and that salvation can be found in any or all of these churches. However, Jude said **the faith** has been "once for all delivered unto the saints" (Jude 3). Peter said that through the knowledge of God and of Jesus our Lord, "His divine power **has given** to us all things that pertain to life and godliness, through the knowledge of Him who called us by glory and virtue" (2 Peter 1:3). These passages tell us that the gospel had been completed in the days of the New Testament and that there is no need for any denomination that came after that time. Any church that came into existence after this time cannot be the church of the New Testament. Jesus died for "THE CHURCH," not a church or some churches. He did not die for the denominations of the world, but for the church He promised to build (Matthew 16:18). This is why we stress the importance of restoring New Testament Christianity.

What Does The Bible Say About Salvation?

Notice we do not ask the question, "What does a particular church teach about salvation?" The reason for this is that no church has the divine right to teach anything about salvation other than what is revealed in the Bible. Many study their Bibles and twist the scriptures to suit them, and determine this to be the answer to their personal search for salvation. Some say they are saved by the love of God, others by mercy or grace. Some say they are saved by obedience, some by the blood of Christ. Some say they are saved by faith, others by repenting and asking Jesus into their heart. Some require a "spiritual experience" while some believe acknowledgement of Jesus as their savior is all that is needed.

How confusing when different churches teach different things about salvation! How do we navigate through these waters of confusion and uncertainty? We do so by looking at what is revealed to us in the Bible, the inspired word of God.

The Bible teaches that man's salvation involves God's part and man's part. Both parts are necessary for salvation. If we are open minded and receptive to God's word, we will accept what God has to say about this matter and turn from the doctrines of men.

God's Part in Man's Salvation

God Himself saves man. We are justified (declared guiltless) by God through faith (Romans 3:25, 30; 8:33). Faith is produced by God's word (Romans 10:17).

Mercy saves man. How blessed we are that God's "merciful kindness is great toward us" (Psalm 117:2), and that "according to His mercy He saved us, through the washing of regeneration and renewing of the Holy Spirit" (Titus 3:5).

Sending Christ saves man. The Bible says that "He [Jesus] will save His people from their sins" (Matthew 1:21), and that "the Son of Man has come to seek and to save that which was lost" (Luke 19:10).

The shedding of Christ's blood saves man. We are "justified by His blood" and "saved from wrath through Him" (Romans 5:9). Jesus, in instituting the Lord's Supper, said, "For this is My blood of the new covenant, which is shed for many for the remission of sins" (Matthew 26:28); and in Revelation 1:5, John writes, "and from Jesus Christ, the faithful witness, the firstborn from the dead, and the ruler over the kings of the earth. To Him who loved us and washed us from our sins in His own blood."

The sending of the gospel saves man. The gospel is the power that God uses to bring us to salvation. "For I am not ashamed of the gospel of Christ, for it is the power of God to salvation for everyone who believes, for the Jew first and also for the Greek. For in it the righteousness of God is revealed from faith to faith; as it is written, "'The just shall live by faith'" (Romans 1:16-17). Paul said that it "pleased God through the foolishness of preaching to save those who believe" (1 Corinthians 1:21). Paul plainly stated that the gospel saves us in 1 Corinthians 15:1-2, where he says "Moreover, brethren, I declare to you the gospel which I preached to you, which also you received and in which you stand, by which also you are saved, if you hold fast that word which I preached to you—unless you believed in vain." Paul also said to Timothy that the scriptures were able to make him "wise for salvation through faith which is in Christ Jesus" (2 Timothy 3:15). When Peter came to the household of Cornelius, he stated that he had come to "tell you words by which you and all your household will be saved" (Acts 11:14).

God's grace saves man. It is God's grace "that brings salvation" and "has appeared to all men" (Titus 2:11). We are justified by His grace (Titus 3:7). It is "by grace you have been saved and that is "through faith" (Ephesians 2:5; 2:8).

God's longsuffering saves man. God wants all men to be saved. For this reason God is longsuffering toward us. Peter says, "And consider that the longsuffering of our Lord is salvation—as also our beloved brother Paul, according to the wisdom given to him, has written to you" (2 Peter 3:15).

Perhaps there are other things we can find in the Bible that mention God's part of salvation, but let us now look at man's part in salvation. As we do so, let us remember that we are not to "pick and choose" from those things God says, but we are to do all the things that God requires of us.

Man's Part in Salvation

The Bible teaches that we must hear the Word of God. It is through the word of God, the Bible, that we can understand the will of God for man. Paul said "Faith comes by hearing and hearing by the word of God" (Romans 10:17). We cannot know what we must do to be saved unless we can read what we must do in the Bible. Therefore, Bible study is necessary to know God's will for man.

Man must have faith in the Word of God. It is not enough to hear God's word; we must believe that it is God's revealed message to mankind. Jesus said, "He who believes and is baptized will be saved; but he who does not believe will be condemned" (Mark 16:16). The Hebrew writer said, "But without faith it is impossible to please Him, **for he who comes to God must believe that He is**, and that He is a rewarder of those who diligently seek Him" (Hebrews 11:6).

Man must repent of his sins. In Luke 13:3, Jesus said, "Except you repent you shall all likewise perish". He again repeated this in verse five. The Bible teaches that God requires "all men everywhere to repent" (Acts 17:30). When we repent, we determine to turn away from the sins that separate us from God and have genuine sorrow for our sins.

Man must confess Christ. Confession of Christ as Savior is a part of the gospel plan of salvation. The Bible teaches, "For with the heart one believes unto righteousness, and with the mouth confession is made unto salvation" (Romans 10:10).

Man must obey God's will. God has always required obedience from man. Even Jesus was obedient to the will of God: "though He was a Son, yet He learned obedience by the things which He suffered. And having been perfected, He became the author of eternal salvation to all who obey Him" (Heb. 5:8-9).

Man must be baptized for remission of sins. People in most denominations agree with all that has been said up to this point, and then fail when it comes to obeying the requirement of being baptized for remission of sins. The passages that teach this are numerous and there is not room in this printing to pursue all of them. However, notice some of the passages where God, through the Holy Spirit, tells how one becomes a Christian.

Jesus, before ascending back to heaven, said to his disciples, "'Go therefore and make disciples of all the nations, baptizing them in the name of the Father and of the Son and of the Holy Spirit, teaching them to observe all things that I have commanded you; and lo, I am with you always, even to the end of the age." Amen'" (Matthew 28:19-20).

Peter, in the first gospel sermon, said, "… "Repent, and let every one of you be baptized in the name of Jesus Christ for the remission of sins; and you shall receive the gift of the Holy Spirit" (Acts 2:38).

Later on, in the first epistle of Peter, Peter said that baptism saves us. "There is also an antitype which now saves us—baptism (not the removal of the filth of the flesh, but the answer of a good conscience toward God), through the resurrection of Jesus Christ" (1 Peter 3:21).

When the apostle Paul recounted his conversion, he said that Ananias came to him and said, "And now why are you waiting? Arise and be baptized, and wash away your sins, calling on the name of the Lord" (Acts 22:16).

Paul also said that it is through baptism that we put on Christ. "For as many of you as were baptized into Christ have put on Christ" (Galatians 3:27).

Denominational preachers will try to dismiss these scriptures as unimportant and baptism for remission of sins as unnecessary. But read for yourself what GOD SAYS!

Man must endure to be saved. Jesus knew that many would start on the road to heaven and then fall away. Therefore He said, "But he who endures to the end shall be saved" (Matthew 24:13). This is repeated in Mark 13:13: "And you will be hated by all for My name's sake. But he who endures to the end shall be saved". Paul, using the analogy of a race, points out that salvation is for those who "finished the race" and "have kept the faith." Those who do so will receive a "crown of righteousness" (2 Timothy 4:7-8).

Man must love the truth in order to be saved. Paul talks of those that will perish because "they did not receive the love of the truth, that they might be saved" (2 Thessalonians 2:10).

The church of Christ is a group of Christians meeting in a given location who have joined themselves together to worship God according to the New Testament pattern. The New Testament church had no denominational name or headquarters. It did not have members of any man-made denominational organization, conference, synod, or association. The New Testament church was made up of Christians trying to serve God in the manner prescribed by God's word. They are not perfect and infallible, but know that God is, and that they must strive to serve Him in order to have salvation. They are concerned about having scriptural authority for the things they do.

The organization of the New Testament church has elders, deacons and saints (Philippians 1:1) The elders have oversight of the congregation and "shepherd the flock" (Acts 20:28; 1 Peter 5:2).

The New Testament church did not support any of the man-made, quasi-church institutions that have become so much a part of many churches today. The New Testament church was not involved in sports, parties, church socials, or any other activities for which we cannot find scriptural authority. We are to follow the biblical pattern of the work of the church, that being the preaching of the gospel (Acts 13:1-3), edifying of the saints (Ephesians 4:12, 16), and providing benevolence for needy saints (1 Corinthians 16:1-2). The Bible teaches that, as individuals, we are to "do good to all, especially to those who are of the household of faith" (Galatians 6:10).

Final Word

Worship is an obligation that man has toward God. However, man should not look at worship as a mere obligation, but consider worship a beautiful privilege of honoring and glorifying the One who made man and the one from whom all spiritual blessings flow. Certainly it is God who gives "every good gift and every perfect gift" (James 1:17). It is the will of God that man might have eternal salvation. He gives you spiritual birth through "the word of truth," and when you lay "aside all filthiness and overflow of wickedness," and "receive with meekness the implanted word," it "is able to save your souls" (James 1:21)

Man has often tried to improve on God's plan and has succeeded in making a mess of Christ's church. Most practice things in worship that are unrecognizable when compared with the church of the New Testament. Man needs to remember that the "foolishness of God is wiser than men, and the weakness of God is stronger than men" (1 Corinthians 1:25). Isn't it about time that we returned to the Bible for instruction as to how to worship God, rather than changing worship in order to make man feel good about his worship? As stated previously, the real problem is that man is now the center of worship in many churches. The worship service is centered on what man wants and desires in worship, rather than what God desires. May man repent of this wrong.

www.ingramcontent.com/pod-product-compliance
Lightning Source LLC
LaVergne TN
LVHW091554060526
838200LV00036B/835